THE COMPLETE
CORVETTE

Introduction

Chevrolet was about as well placed to produce a sports car in 1953 as Caterpillar would be today. They lacked the experience, the reputation, the engine, the transmission; their dealers were completely unused to sports cars, and it was uncertain if there was really a market out there in middle America. What they did have was a dealer in every town and city across the nation, first class technical and research facilities, excellent manufacturing, and a very well known brand. They had the foresight to invest in the best engineers, designers, and stylists, the capital to invest in and develop an entirely new technology for making plastic bodies, and most important of all a great new V8 engine ready for production in 1955.

The Chevrolet Corvette is by far the most popular and successful two-seater sports car ever built. On July 2, 1992 the millionth Corvette was assembled and annual sales have exceeded 20,000 every full sales year since.

This book celebrates the 50th anniversary of a car which is seven years into production of its 5th generation model, a car which is clearly superior to any of its forebears but carries on the same family tradition of a torquey V8 motor in a superbly styled and yet practical body. Always the focused 2-seater with the powerful engine and lightweight fiberglass body, the Corvette has never been permitted to dilute its image by incorporating a second row of seats.

The first ten years saw steady improvement after a shaky start, more power, a new V8, better manual transmissions and ever increasing sales and popularity. Then the magnificent independent rear suspension second series model was introduced in 1963, gained disc brakes and the optional big block 7-liter engines, and Corvette became a world standard

ultra high performance icon of the mid-sixties. When a government that had apparently not even one car enthusiast in its ranks dealt the double blow of both stringent exhaust emissions and demanding Federal bumper and crash protection legislation at the same time, the Corvette was ingeniously adapted to pass the tests. Refining a ten-year-old design the Corvette marched on towards its Silver Anniversary, and then its highest-ever annual sales figures in 1979. In the next fifteen years, the Corvette showcased brilliant engine management systems, which not only met and exceeded ever more rigorous emissions and fuel economy legislation, but which made its V8 more powerful and faster than ever before. Between 1980 and 1990 the Corvette's maximum speed increased by 35% and its high speed fuel economy by 50%.

The extraordinary thing is that this long tradition of great sports cars has not been the product of an enthusiastic family, a car-mad industrialist, or a motor racing dynasty, but has been made by Chevrolet, the cheap family car division of General Motors—for most of the 20th century the world's largest corporation and one of its most profitable.

It is even more extraordinary because the Corvette has never really fitted into the Chevrolet model range, and has always been the most expensive car it made, usually costing half as much again as the most luxurious full size car in the range. It is also a tiny part of the Chevrolet range; in 1971 for instance less than 1.5% of all Chevrolet production was Corvettes. It was probably a money loser for its first seven years and has remained acceptably profitable ever since. The Corporation does not tolerate losses for long but along with the small block V8, this car transformed Chevrolet's staid image.

Above: The new 1953 Corvette.

Of the great minds behind the Corvette, Harley Earl, a real car enthusiast and Californian, who in 1927 had set up GM's Art & Colour Studio was well aware of the increasing interest in European sports cars, particularly the stunning English Jaguar XK120. This was probably the starting point for the prototype General Motors 2-seater. The Jaguar had been available since 1949, shared the 102 inch wheel base, had the same sharp definition of its cockpit area, looked good without the wire wheels that normally said "sports car," and apparently survived on the road with rudimentary bumpers.

The proposed GM sports car started with a considerable advantage over the Jaguar because it had no need to carry the old world symbolism incorporated into a vertical radiator grille. And though of comparable length and wheel base, the Corvette's track was a full 6 inches wider.

Harley Earl's talented team included Henry Lauve who had been with GM styling since 1939, and was probably the principal stylist of the prototype. The semi-pontoon fenders with high mounted recessed head lamps and a bulbous fin finishing the rear were his trademark. Lauve had developed the wraparound windshield of the fabulous 1951 Le Sabre dream car and the new project, would be the first, and last, production car with this dramatic feature. Carl Renner had joined GM in 1945 and was a master of the toothy air intake grille.

Left: Harley Earl.

Below: Jaguar XK 120.

Engineer Robert F McLean is credited with the basic layout of the design. He started by placing the bucket seats as far back as possible, he sketched in the steering wheel and instrument panel, and then placed the motor as close to this as could, and low to the ground. The standard front suspension cross member went in front of the motor, establishing the 102 inch wheel base.

A full size plaster model of the proposed car was finished by June 1952 and shown to the new Chevrolet chief engineer, Ed Cole. He wanted the as yet unnamed roadster for his Chevrolet division, and must have foreseen that the compact small block V8 his team, led by ex-Cadillac engineer Harry Barr, was developing would be the ideal power plant.

The task of making it all work passed to English suspension expert, engineer Maurice Olley, originator of double wishbone suspension, and by now head of Research and Development. He was to design a chassis using as many production parts as possible, and make the new car handle as well as it looked. He had pioneered the use of a threaded bush in each pivot to give precise location which was carried on into the Corvette's front suspension, and the sway bar to control the roll which was the initial problem with independent front suspension. Using only production parts he managed to get it right immediately; exactly the same chassis with only improved rear axle location went on to an outstanding 8th place at Le Mans in 1960—still the equal to the best ever result for the multi million dollar C5R at the 2002 running of the 24 hour French endurance race.

By using the corporate front suspension assembly that he had developed, a radiator inclined rearward, a steering column that was almost horizontal by prevailing standards, a rear axle mounted onto thoughtfully located semi elliptic multi-leaf springs and tying the components together with a fully boxed and diagonally braced frame, Olley was able to provide the prototype with handling and road holding that was unlike any American car of the time.

By now officially a Chevrolet, a suitable name had to be found for the new sports car, which was rapidly

Above: Ed Cole.

Opposite: Cutaway of the 1989 375 bhp 32 valve ZR1, as tested by the press, but finally launched as a 1990 model.

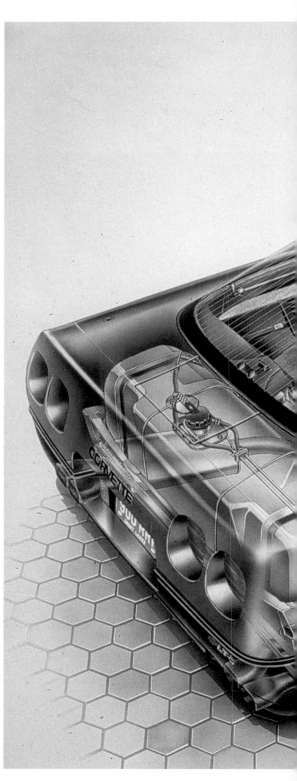

becoming a running reality. Many names had been considered and rejected when Myron Scott, a Chevrolet public relations executive, heard that the board had decided that the car's name should begin with the letter C. He claimed that he looked through the Cs in a dictionary, and quickly found Corvette. He liked the sound of the word and the association of a fast and maneuverable naval vessel with the new sports car, submitted the name to Ed Cole who had by now adopted the car as his own and the Chevrolet Corvette as a brand was born.

Having adopted Harley Earl's sports car, Ed Cole was now obliged to use the only performance engine that Chevrolet had, the 235.5 cubic inch straight six. This was an uprated version of the 216.5 offered only as an automatic, and by careful tuning the engine was able to make 150bhp. It was logical to build the show car as an automatic, Chevrolet's Powerglide was one of the best in the industry, and as any hot-rodder knows, it is much easier to build a one-off car if you can dispense with the complication of clutch pedals and linkages.

The hood kept its low line by the use of triple side draft carburetors, a header tank for the low mounted radiator was mounted along the left side of the engine valve cover and the water pump was modified to mount lower.

The new Corvette prototype was first shown to the public at the GM Motorama, held at the Waldorf Astoria Hotel in January 1953. The reception of the Corvette was tremendous and Chevrolet, who need never have revealed that the body was made of plastic, made the most of the publicity that the new material generated as the Motorama Show moved from city to city. The day after the opening of the show in New York, GM president Harlow Curtice announced that the new sports car would go into production in June. At the end of March 1953, after wavering between steel and fiberglass, the decision was finally made to go with the latter and to establish a production line capable of building 10,000 cars per year. They did not know then that it would take until 1960 to achieve that target.

SPECIFICATIONS

Wheel-base 102"
Length 13' 11"
Width 5' 10"
Weight 2850 lbs
Transmission 2 speed auto
Brakes 11" drum
Engine 235 six
Compression 8.0
Gross Horse Power 150

1953

Just over five months after the prototype had been unveiled at the New York GM Motorama in January, the first Corvette rolled off the short Flint assembly line on June 30, 1953. It was a genuine mass-produced sports car and certainly the most advanced produced in any American assembly plant on that summer Tuesday in June. It would become an icon for millions of Americans, most yet unborn.

That Polo White 1953 Corvette with the Sportsman Red interior was almost identical to the Motorama car. The Corvette script was missing below the round crossed flags emblem, resulting in a cleaner front end and a practical chrome side strip now extended down the sides, protecting the body and covering the seam where the upper body was riveted and bonded to the lower. Another improvement was the loss of the small scoops at the top rear of the front fenders, though these would return on the 1956.

The convertible top needed to be simple and light for easy folding into the limited storage compartment, so it used only two intermediate bows that gave a rather angular appearance when erected. The ingenious lifting rear bow allowed the top to be fully hidden when stowed under the lifting rear deck, a system that became a Corvette tradition and was not copied by others until some thirty years later.

This first Corvette production operation, with a line just six cars long, was in a disused customer delivery building on Van Slyke Road on the south side of Flint, some fifty miles north of Detroit. Cars were produced at about three per day and three hundred were finally built by Christmas 1953, when production was moved to St Louis, Missouri.

While the very earliest bodies were hand-laid, all of the 62 panels that made up a Corvette were

being formed under pressure between matched metal dies by the time that production transferred to St Louis. It was a two stage process; an operator used a hand-held gun to simultaneously spray resin, hardener and chopped fiberglass thread to build up a preform panel, which was rotated to ensure that the chopped fibers were laid in all directions, making the final panel stronger. The preform, now like a bulky mass of matting, was run through a continuous oven to semi-cure the resin, and then placed in the bottom half of the matched dies. A second layer of fine mat was placed on the top and a measured amount of resin poured on to the preform. The metal dies were then closed together under great pressure, while they were heated by internal electrical or hot water coils. A gel coat was not used in this process, the high molding pressure ensuring that the panel was uniformly dense.

After about three minutes the dies were reopened and the cured panel was removed with the characteristic perfect finish on both sides, only requiring final trimming. From the very beginning the Corvette never had a bad reputation for fiberglass problems, and never suffered from porosity, starring, delamination, osmosis or any of the other familiar woes.

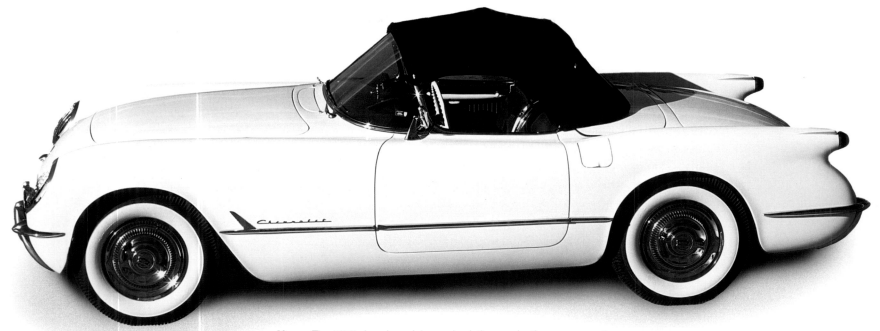

Above: The 1953 chassis mainly used existing production components.

Below: The 235 cubic inch ohv six cylinder made only 150 bhp, despite triple Carter carbs.

Above: The constrictive convertible top dropped into a storage space, and was covered by hinged deck lid panel.

Right: Wire mesh head light covers were a clever styling trick that shouted "sports car!"

SPECIFICATIONS

Wheel-base 102"
Length 13' 11"
Width 5' 10"
Weight 2850 lbs
Transmission 2 speed auto
Brakes 11" drum
Engine 235 six
Compression 8.0
Gross Horse Power 150-155

1954

The St. Louis-built 1954 looked very little different to the 1953. Polo White was still the most popular color, striking in an age when an all-white car was unusual, but 300 1954s were finished in Pennant Blue with beige interior, 100 in Sportsman Red with red interior and just 4 in Black with red upholstery. Externally the only obvious changes were the new beige convertible top replacing black, and later in production, longer exhaust tailpipe extensions, incorporating deflectors to direct the exhaust gas to the road. These were the first evidence of Zora Arkus-Duntov's influence on the Corvette.

Duntov's kind of practical can-do background and racing experience—he had also raced Porsches in Europe—was exactly what was needed by Chevrolet to get their uncertain sports car licked into shape. Determined to work for General Motors, he had been hired by the Chevrolet division in 1954 and almost immediately got himself involved with the Corvette. He did not stop at experimenting with exhaust outlets but went on to become chief engineer and the single most important figure in the first twenty years of the car's history.

Chevrolet could put together 50 cars a day at the large St. Louis plant, but it was soon obvious that an embarrassing number of unsold cars had accumulated. In July 1954 production was cut back to 300 cars per month, and by the end of the year only 3,640 cars had been built, of which more than a quarter were still unsold. The problem was that the list price, including required options, was twice that of a basic Chevrolet with the same engine, and nor far short of a new V8 Cadillac, which had 210 horsepower, proper side windows and external door handles.

Management were clearly ready to drop the whole sporty car experiment, but the Corvette was saved by the launch of Ford's Thunderbird—itself a response to the Motorama Corvette, an excellent two seater convertible with a V8 and a choice of automatic or manual transmission. If Ford was intending to open up a new market for personal cars, then GM would persevere with its own contender rather than relinquish their stake in a potential growth sector.

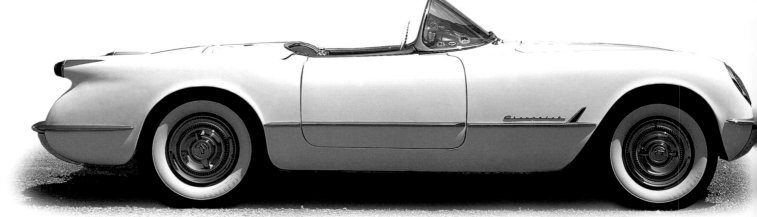

Above: Zora Arkus-Duntov.

Above: 1954 was available in colours other than white.

Above: A deck lid concealed the folded top.

Right: 1954 tops were beige.

SPECIFICATIONS

Wheel-base 102"
Length 13' 11"
Width 5' 10"
Weight 2910 lbs
Transmission 2 speed auto
  or 3 speed manual
Brakes 11" drum
Engines
  Base 235 six
  Compression 8.0
  Gross Horse Power 155

  Optional 265 V8
  Compression 8.0
  Gross hp 195

1955

Way back in October 1953 work had started to adapt the new small block V8 to the Corvette, and for 1955 the original shaped car was given the V8 engine that it deserved. Externally, a gold V superimposed on the V of Chevrolet on each front fender showed that the V8 was installed. Only about 625 1955s with this engine were built, making this model one of the rarest and therefore expensive of all Corvettes—but even if they had built ten times that number it would still be just as desirable.

Other changes for 1955 were few, in particular extra colors were offered for the body, interior and top including Corvette Copper, Gypsy Red and Harvest Gold. The last came with a dark green convertible top and a

yellow interior and yellow wheels. A white vinyl soft top was also introduced, forerunner of a change to this material in 1956.

The chassis frame design was typical of the era and it is interesting to note that its diagonal cross bracing precluded lowering either the seats or the footwells. This directly led to two criticisms of the design. Firstly the seats were too high, bad for tall drivers particularly with the top up, and secondly the driver's feet were too high up for long distance comfort.

It will be easily deduced from the above that the Corvette was a car waiting for an engine and it was given that engine in 1955. Whenever the Corvette is compared

Above Left: The steering wheel reflected the Corvette's sedan origins.

Above Right: Destined to become the world's biggest selling automobile engine —1955 small-block V8.

to other sports cars, two key features stand out over 40 years and these are the features that have made it the best selling two-seat sports car ever. They are the durable double-die molded fiberglass body, and the torquey, powerful and simple V8 motor. The 1953 and 1954 simply lacked this motor, and the six cylinder could not provide exciting performance. Those who thought the six too slow or dull were rewarded in January 1955 with the announcement of the optional 265 cubic inch V8. The effect was dramatic. Suddenly the Corvette was transformed from an interesting-looking, fiberglass-bodied, two-seater which was a disappointment to drive, into a true sports car, a car

with all the power you dare use under the right foot and a little bit extra as well.

Sports cars have to be about driver satisfaction. They need to be light, or if like the Corvette they are quite heavy, then they need a motor that has sufficient power to make them feel light. The new 265 V8 had power to spare, 40 horsepower more than the 155 of the six, and 35 lb.ft more torque at 3000rpm. The V8 felt livelier too, the stroke of the six was 1/16 inch short of 4 inches while the V8 was only 3 inches and that combined with larger piston area meant instant response and higher revs.

Left: "V" in Chevrolet denoted V8 motor.

SPECIFICATIONS

Wheel-base 102"
Length 14' 0"
Width 5' 11"
Weight 2970 lbs
Transmission 2 speed auto
or 3 speed manual
Brakes 11" drum
Engines
  Base 265 V8
  Compression 8.0
  Gross Horse Power 210

  Option 469 265 V8
  Compression 9.25
  Gross Horse Power 225

  Option 449 265 V8
  Compression 9.25
  Gross Horse Power 240

1956

By the middle of the decade the Corvette was looking a little slab-sided and plain. The curves of the body were somewhat soft and ill defined and the body shape did not take full advantage of the potential of fiberglass construction. The car had been unchanged for three model years, at a time when all models from every American manufacturer were restyled every year.

The 1956 Corvette had to be something very special indeed, particularly because it was now Chevrolet's most expensive car as well as its image builder and styling flagship. Those who were close at the time reported that the facelift was done very quickly, once the decision had been taken to continue production and launch a 1956. The restyled car now appealed to a more enthusiastic and critical breed of buyer, and established the tradition that would make Corvette the best-selling sports car of the twentieth century.

There is no doubt that Ford's Thunderbird spurred Chevrolet to fight back with a radically improved Corvette. First seen at a Detroit Auto Show in February 1954, it was in production by September 1954. Design work is said to have started on the Thunderbird within a month of the first 1953 Motorama in New York. With an overhead valve V8 available, and one of the most romantic names ever attached to a car, they must have known that they had a winner. Indeed, it sold over 16,000 units in the twelve months of the 1955 model year, compared to a total of just 4640 Corvettes produced in three years by Chevrolet.
It was a better-looking car and even today

much nicer to drive. Fortunately, Ford would go on to mess it up in 1958, making the T-Bird 1000 pounds heavier and giving it four seats, leaving the Corvette unchallenged as America's only mass produced two-seater for the next four decades.

The new 1956 body fitted the same chassis frame, but every panel was different and changed to achieve a tauter and more eager appearance. The headlights were brought forward and emphasized with their own round, chromium-plated rims and the parking lamps were moved directly beneath them. The hood was given twin longitudinal bulges, which helped to stiffen this panel. Behind the front wheel opening, and running back into the door, was a sculpted scoop, generally now called a cove and referred to in contemporary advertising as an indent. This was picked out with a stainless steel molding, clipped to the body, which also surrounded the front wheel arch. It could be painted in silver or beige, depending on the body color, for an additional $19.40.

After three years of production in which the doors could only be opened by reaching past the side curtains to the internal door release knobs, now there were external chrome plated handles and door locks that were conveniently operated by the ignition key. Wind up flat glass door windows, with the option of electric power

operation, replaced the side curtains, making the '55 Corvette the last American production car in more than fifty years to use them.

Atop each of the front fenders was the only non-functional styling gimmick on the car, an air scoop the same as was seen on the 1953 Motorama show car, but which hadn't made production on the 53–55. The wheel openings in both the front and rear fenders on the '56 had the plain crisp cut edge, which not only identified the body as being made of fiberglass but became a Corvette trade mark. The '53 body had been designed to be fabricated from pressed steel if required, so the wheel openings carried the characteristic rolled shape of metal construction. The effect of the plain edge was to emphasize the elegant shape of the new car, and this was accentuated by the swept back rear of each wheel opening.

The "futurist" rear light pods were removed and instead the rear lights were neatly dropped into scoops in the reshaped fenders. The previous model had long suffered from exhaust fumes being drawn back into the cabin, so now the exhaust outlets were in the rear of the fender pontoons so that waste gasses could be carried away more easily.

The bumpers now incorporated an over rider above the newly-positioned exhaust pipe outlet, reaching up the center line of the fender. Otherwise, the bumpers were no stronger than previously, in contrast with other 1956 domestic cars whose bumpers were so strong that they were used to jack the car for tire changing.

The folding convertible top shape was changed by the introduction of two additional bows, which not only improved its appearance and reduced its overall height, but also made it easier to erect. However, it still restricted side vision for tall drivers and left a large blind spot

between the side and back windows. There was a color choice of black, beige or white vinyl material for the top.

Power operation of the convertible top was listed as an option, but at least the first 2500 cars built for the 1956 model year all had it fitted as standard, the manual operation not being available again until the end of May of that year. More than 77% of '56s were fitted with the hydraulic convertible top, but by 1962 this figure had shrunk to a mere 2.4%. The power system used a trunk-mounted 12 volt electric motor powered hydraulic pump, two solenoid valves, one hydraulic cylinder to control the convertible top cover, two cylinders to power the top itself, two convertible top cover limit switches, two limit switches for the top itself and two safety switches to prevent operation with either the trunk open or the top cover latched shut. Before using the dash-mounted switch, the driver was required to unlatch the top cover and release the two upholstery tabs, hold the rear bow of the top forward after the top was raised to allow the return of the top lid, and at the end of the sequence to latch the front bow and perhaps struggle to reach back and fasten the rear of the top. Since not much more work was required to lift the top manually, it was not surprising that in many cases rams were released from the frame as soon as the system gave trouble. Without the power option the top was still very easy to erect, and with practice could be stowed without the driver leaving his seat.

The optional fiberglass detachable hard top was offered either as a $215.20 addition or as a no cost alternative to the soft top, and featured a beautifully designed

quarter window behind the door window for all-round vision. Mounted at the front with latches similar to the convertible top, it was screwed at the rear to the deck lid in three positions. Like all Corvette hard tops since, this was a careful and masterful piece of automotive design,

subtly changing the appearance of the convertible to which it was fitted. A particularly appealing feature of the hard top is that, when properly installed, it can be swung into a vertical position to impress onlookers, by releasing the three latches to allow loading behind the seats.

Above Left: Seat design was beautifully integrated with the external body shape.

Above Right: The new 1956 steering wheel, unique to Corvette.

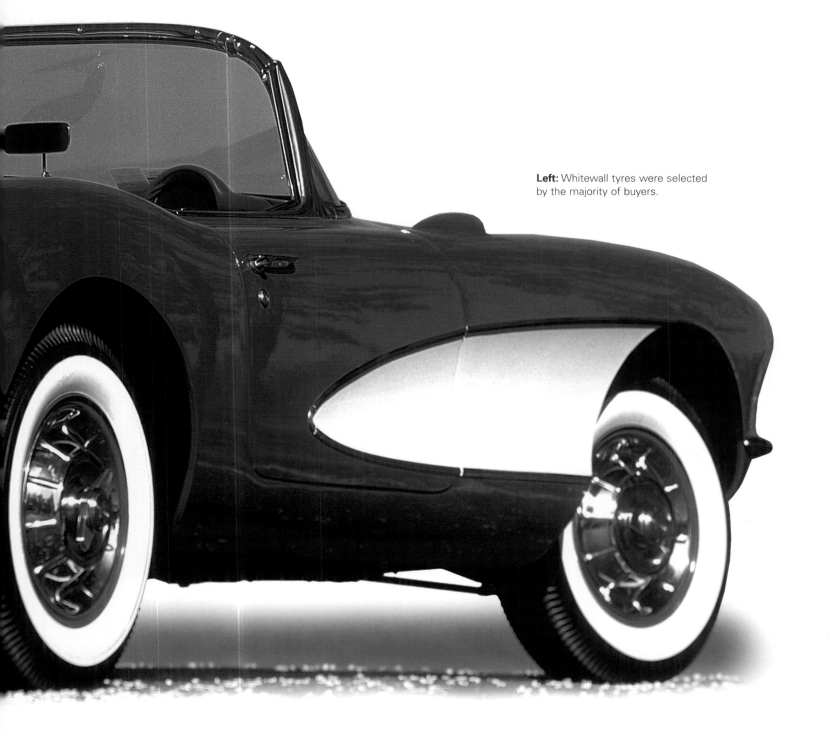

Left: Whitewall tyres were selected by the majority of buyers.

1957

Externally on a basic-optioned car there were no changes for the 1957—the car was a true carryover from 1956. However, if the optional hardtop was fitted, then an immediate difference was apparent at the front of the hardtop, where there was now a 2 inch wide stainless steel header trim in place of the anodized and sometimes painted trim on the '56 hardtop. But 1957 has become one of those milestone years because it saw the introduction of three important performance features—a more powerful 283 cubic inch motor to replace the 265 and the options of 4-speed manual transmission and fuel injection. The extra capacity of the engine was achieved by increasing the bore to $3\frac{7}{8}$ inches while retaining the short 3 inch stroke, making this lusty V8 even more over-square and lively than previously.

The Borg-Warner 3-speed manual transmission had first been fitted in 1955 to some 75 cars, then to two out of three of 1956 production. By 1957 only 21% of Corvettes were ordered with the 2-speed automatic Powerglide, and the optional Borg-Warner T10 4-speed now helped mark the Corvette's position as a true sports car, but propelling the car to true world class technology was the new Rochester fuel injection. Although fitted to less than 17% of production in 1957, it had a halo effect that has never been forgotten, particularly since Chevrolet continued with it through 1965 and were quick to reintroduce it in electronic form in 1982. Fuel injection not only made the engine more powerful, but also banished one of the banes of the

Corvette racers—fuel surge in the carburetor float chamber. This has long been a problem where a car with a four-barrel carburetor is driven hard round a bend, and a centrifugal force of up to 1g forces the fuel to the wall of the float chamber. Fuel injection solved this problem and improved the power and responsiveness of the engine at the same time.

The top-performing engine combined fuel injection with a 10.5:1 compression ratio, and with the Duntov solid lifter competition cam to give 283bhp. The output of this motor was believed to have been more like 290 horsepower, but 283 was the number chosen, so that it could claim one horsepower per cubic inch. No other Corvette power output has ever been advertised to single digit accuracy, indeed engine dynamometers are still not that accurate, particularly if one is averaging a number of full power passes on the machine.

SPECIFICATIONS

Wheel-base 102"
Length 14' 10"
Width 6' 1"
Weight 3135 lbs
Transmission 2 speed auto
  or 3 speed manual
  or 4 speed manual
Brakes 11" drum
Engines
  Base 283 V8
  Compression 9.5
  Gross Horse Power 230

  Option 469 283 V8
  Compression 9.5
  Gross Horse Power 245

  Option 469C 283 V8
  Compression 9.5
  Gross Horse Power 270

  Option 579 283 V8
    fuel injection
  Compression 9.5
  Gross Horse Power 250

  Option 579D 283 V8
    fuel injection
  Compression 10.5
  Gross Horse Power 290

1958

By 1958 the US economy was booming, the national mood was one of self confidence, General Motors was as successful as ever and its cars were getting bigger, lower and wider. The Corvette was now the Chevrolet image builder and had to reflect something of the corporate look.

Like arch rivals Ford, and almost all of the GM range, Chevrolet adopted quad headlamps for 1958 and the Corvette had to have them too. The need for annual innovation was paramount, particularly because 1958 was GM's golden anniversary year. The '57 was an almost perfect shape but if it had been left as it was it would have soon become old fashioned, for these were times of rapid change, growth and innovation. General Motors Styling Staff were constantly presented with an almost impossible task by the annual model change. If they produced perfection, they had to improve it for the following model year, but the limited production Corvette was happily allowed to run for years without major change, to the continuing joy of parts specialists everywhere.

The changes for 1958 were considerable and increased the length of the car by 9 inches, the width by 2 inches and added 200 pounds to the overall weight. Where the 1956–57 model's bumpers had been skimpy and bolted to the fiberglass, now they were immense and bolted through to the frame. On the production line they had to be fitted after the body was dropped on to the frame rather than before it. At the rear, the exhaust now exited through an oval aperture in a complex chromed bumper that stretched from license plate to wheel opening on either side. As on Cadillacs of the era, steam and acid from the exhaust gasses would rust away the bumpers quickly unless extensions were fitted to the tailpipes. The bumper exhaust outlet was a great styling feature, and use of the exhaust pipe as a design element has continued with most Corvettes to the present day.

The front of the car was cleverly restyled to accommodate the four 5 $\frac{3}{4}$ inch sealed beam headlights. They were a real improvement for night driving; the outer sealed beam units contained dipped and main beam filaments, the inner pair were single filament and were lit only when main beam was selected with the floor mounted switch. Below the quad lights were new dummy grilles—although not dummy if the Heavy Duty Brakes and suspension option was ordered—and these served as the inlet for the brake cooling ducts. At a glance the main grille appeared to be similar to the previous year's, but it was narrower and had only nine, and not thirteen, of the same teeth. There were new emblems at front and rear; they were given visual depth by making them up of four separate pieces—a bezel, seal, clear emblem, and lower dished reflector—and fitted into holes in the nose and trunk lid. The bezels rotated at 90 degrees to fit the different body curves.

Above: Seat belts were factory installed in all Corvettes from 1958. The new dash put all the gauges in front of the driver.

Below: The new 4 headlamp body was 2″ wider than the previous body.

Right: Only the 1958 had the twin chrome plated trunk lid ribs.

Above: Fuel injection would be available until 1965, but carbureted 283s like this one were much easier to live with.

SPECIFICATIONS

Wheel-base 102"
Length 14' 10"
Width 6' 1"
Weight 3135 lbs
Transmission 2 speed auto
    or 3 speed manual
    or 4 speed manual
Brakes 11" drum
Engines
  Base 283 V8
  Compression 9.5
  Gross Horse Power 230

  Option 469 283 V8
  Compression 9.5
  Gross Horse Power 245

  Option 469C 283 V8
  Compression 9.5
  Gross Horse Power 270

  Option 579 283 V8
    fuel injection
  Compression 9.5
  Gross Horse Power 250

  Option 579D 283 V8
    fuel injection
  Compression 10.5
  Gross Horse Power 290

1959

There were the new vents behind the front wheels, trimmed with three chromed spears on either side, effectively filling in part of the side cove, and restoring the true shape to the rear of the front wheel opening, when compared to the 1957. They served no air outlet function—air coming into the engine compartment through the grill was more than adequately vented through the open underside of the engine compartment. Once again the coves were surrounded with stainless steel trims and, when the optional two-tone exterior paint was ordered, the whole area inside the trim was painted either silver, ivory or black in 1958, silver or ivory in 1959.

The new hood panel was finished with a series of ridges, probably intended as reinforcement, known to enthusiasts as a washboard. The troublesome pop-out hinges on the hood were replaced with plain hinges, making it easier to adjust the hood so that the front edge did not catch. On the trunk lid there were now two chrome-plated longitudinal ribs, which ran down to meet the bullet bumper ends at either side of the license plate.

Above: The passenger had a grab handle and map tray.

While these suggested to the observer that they might be part of an extra luggage rack system, they were not. For 1959, both the washboard on the hood and the chromed trunk ribs were discarded, improving the appearance for all—except, of course, those who own 1958s today, who will hopefully defend their washboard and ribs. Also at the rear was the new tail light design, which now used a red lens flush with the body, one of the neatest jobs ever to come out of Detroit.

The seats, which for the two previous years had featured a waffle pattern, now had a directional pattern in the center panels, the vinyl material being "pebble grained" and also used for the lining of the optional hard top. For 1959, the seat pleat pattern went from side to side across the center panel.

Anchors for seat belts had been factory installed since 1956, but belts were fitted as standard equipment for the first time in 1958, making the Corvette the first 2-seat production car to be fitted with seat belts as original equipment. Steel gray was the only color available until March 1958, when an additional red was available for the duration of the year. From 1959, a full range of belt colors was introduced.

The door panel was an entirely new design for 1958, with a swirl of embossed bright metal contrasting with an upper vinyl panel, and a carpeted kick panel below. In addition, there were twin safety reflectors to warn following traffic of an open door, and a stout, chrome-plated, vinyl-covered combined door pull and armrest, bolted through the door panel into the door.

Right: 1959 and later wheel covers had ventilation slots.

The new dashboard was one of the all-time classics, triumphantly demonstrating the American ability to make technology stylish. All the disparate elements, which had previously been slung evenly across the instrument panel, were now tightly grouped in less than the span of the steering wheel—apart from the radio and heater controls which were appropriately mid-way between the occupants so that the passenger could adjust them too.

The dominant element in this beautifully designed assemblage was the all-important tachometer, the only instrument of interest to the racing driver; it was racing images that were being so successfully exploited in the Corvette's

advertising. Behind the tachometer, and concentric with it, was the semi-circular speedometer reading to 160mph. The domed upper surface of the instrument binnacle distorted the reflection of passing roadside scenery, adding a delightful dimension to the driver's experience and contrasting with the modern obsession for reflection-free and dull dashes.

SPECIFICATIONS

Wheel-base 102"
Length 14' 10"
Width 6' 1"
Weight 3135 lbs
Transmission 2 speed auto
    or 3 speed manual
    or 4 speed manual
Brakes 11" drum
Engines
    Base 283 V8
    Compression 9.5
    Gross Horse Power 230

    Option 469 283 V8
    Compression 9.5
    Gross Horse Power 245

    Option 469C 283 V8
    Compression 9.5
    Gross Horse Power 270

    Option 579 283 V8
        fuel injection
    Compression 11.0
    Gross Horse Power 250

    Option 579D 283 V8
        fuel injection
    Compression 11.0
    Gross Horse Power 290

1960

The standard 230 horsepower motor for 1958 was 10 horsepower more powerful than its 1957 equivalent. With most years of Corvette it's the base motor that's a honey to drive—not only smooth and easy starting, but with a full 300 lb.ft. of torque at only 3,000 rpm. Of course it's nice to boast about your dual fours or your solid lifters, but for pleasure driving of a 45-year-old car on narrow tires this has to be the ideal motor. The four optional engines now ranged from 245 to 290 hp, two, with dual four barrels and two with fuel injection.

Changes for 1960 were mostly cosmetic. When the two-tone paint option was specified, the coves could be painted in a range of colors to co-ordinate with the main body color. Inside, the seat pleat pattern was altered so it went from fore to aft on the center panel, and the lower panel now wrapped round the front of the seat squab

1961-1962

Wheel-base 102"
Length 14' 9"
Width 5' 11"
Weight 3135 lbs
Transmission 2 speed auto
  or 3 speed manual
  or 4 speed manual
Brakes 11" drum
Engines
  Base 283 V8
  Compression 9.5
  Gross Horse Power 230

  Option 469 283 V8
  Compression 9.5
  Gross Horse Power 245

  Option 468 283 V8
  Compression 9.5
  Gross Horse Power 270

  Option 353 283 V8
    fuel injection
  Compression 11.0
  Gross Horse Power 275

  Option 354 283 V8
    fuel injection
  Compression 11.0
  Gross Horse Power 315

1961

After a slow start, and then eight years of increasing sales and an ever-improving car, the Corvette was emphasizing to the world at large that Chevrolet was now a performance brand, and that the Corvette was the technological showcase. The 283 cubic inch small block was now a serious performance motor, which could be enhanced by optional fuel injection, with numerous race wins to its credit. The eighth place at the Le Mans 24 hour endurance race in 1960, in a basically standard car driven by John Fitch and Bob Grossman, was an outstanding achievement and, though equaled in 2002, has yet to be improved on by the many Corvette entries since.

The Corvette's fiberglass body was also proving to be popular with owners. The styling was still superb and the extra headlamps, larger chrome plated bumpers and more aggressive styling fitted in well with most of the cars at the drive-in in the pre-mall year of 1960. Corvettes have never suffered from the wavy panels that characterized many of the smaller European plastic cars, whose panels were hand laid into female molds rather than pressed between matched dies.

It was planned that 1963 production would be double that of 1960 and the transition was carefully orchestrated. The continuity of the Corvette look would

Above: The 1961 tail presaged the new 1963 Sting Ray, the exhaust discharged behind the rear wheels.

be maintained, so that those seeing the 1963 for the first time, particularly from the rear, would know immediately that this was a Corvette. The styling of the 1963 was based on Bill Mitchell's Sting Ray Racer of 1959, which had won the SCCA C-Modified National Championship in its class in 1960. This was a Dream Car that won races, and now the Dream-Car-to-production-car scenario of 1953 would be repeated ten years later. The rear of the Sting Ray Racer was more race car than road car, but another dream car, the XP-700, had already featured a more production-ready tail with trunk and lights, and a version of this was incorporated into the 1961 Corvette.

From the front, the most obvious change for 1961 was the replacement of the grille teeth by a plain, anodized-aluminum mesh with 14 horizontal bars. The center chromium-plated cross bar used for 1961-2 was smaller than the 1958-60, and lacked the holes for mounting the teeth. This in turn meant that the main front bumpers for 1961-2 were also different at their inner ends. The upper and lower chromium-plated cast main grille shells were essentially the same as the 1958-

60. The 1962 grille was a slightly different pressing to the 1961, and was finished in black to match the black areas within the two outer false grilles.

Further refining the front end appearance was the new emblem, which replaced the previous three piece assembly

Left: This 275 hp fuel injection unit was ribbed, the 315hp was plain.

Below: Pressed aluminum mesh replaced the previous grille teeth.

SPECIFICATIONS

Wheel-base 102"
Length 14' 9"
Width 5' 11"
Weight 3137 lbs
Transmission 2 speed auto
  or 3 speed manual
  or 4 speed manual
Brakes 11" drum
Engines
  Base 327 V8
  Compression 10.5
  Gross Horse Power 250

  Option 583 327 V8
  Compression 10.5
  Gross Horse Power 300

  Option 396 327 V8
  Compression 11.25
  Gross Horse Power 340

  Option 582 327 V8
    fuel injection
  Compression 11.25
  Gross Horse Power 360

1962

that had fitted into a hole in the bodywork. Now a crossed flag, unique to the front of the 1961 model, was fitted to the center of the front panel above the seven individual letters C-O-R-V-E-T-T-E, which were also used on the 1962. Finishing the front end facelift, the head lamp bezels, which had previously been chromium-plated, were now painted in the body color, resulting in a more integrated appearance.

Behind the front wheel opening, the cove with its stainless steel surround and triple spears was unchanged, but the crossed flag emblem was replaced for 1961 by a three-piece unit, comprising a plate with CORVETTE flanked by horizontal chrome ornaments with red infilled above and below.

Behind the doors all the panels were new; the arris which defined the rear of the car extended over the rear wheel openings, while a styled rib or wind-split was introduced running from the front of the deck lid to the rear of the new trunk lid. Devotees of Mitchell style will at once recognize this as one of his trademarks—a similar rib adorned the rear of all 1963–67 Sting Rays and the 1971–72 Buick Riviera boat tail. It can be annoying that a 1961–62 replacement convertible top cannot be fitted to a 1960 car, but the design was undoubtedly improved by that rib. The convertible top had a redesigned rear bow, now aluminum and shaped to accommodate the rib in the deck.

Rear bumpers were entirely new and did not risk damage from the exhaust, whose outlets now terminated unobtrusively downward behind the rear wheels. They were light enough to be fitted to the body prior to the body drop, marking a trend toward lighter bumpers.

Below: Only the 1962 had the fluted cove trim and rocker panel trim.

Left: A detachable hard top had been available since 1956, instead of the soft top or additional to it at extra cost.

Around the rear license plate opening there was a new central bumper, in the form of an inverted U to complete the rear protection.

The four rear lamps started a Corvette tradition that has now endured for more than forty years. The lenses were continued through to Sting Ray production and lasted until 1967, but the four chromium-plated cast housings were unique to these two years.

The final facelift for the Corvette for 1962 saw the complete removal of the brightwork around the cove, and the end of the dual color option. Instead, the cove shape was subtly molded into the fiberglass of the door and front fender, a treatment that matched the revised rear end particularly well. The effect was emphasized by a new fluted cove insert, replacing the spears of the previous four years, and an aluminum rocker molding below the door.

The 1961 engine line up was essentially the same as 1960, though the two fuel-injected versions each gained 25 hp, thanks to the new big valve 11.0:1 "fuelie" cylinder heads. These were initially to have been cast in aluminum, but after difficulties in testing they were finally released in cast iron. The small block engine was offered in 1962 Chevrolet passenger cars in an alternative larger 327 size,

and this was adopted as the basic Corvette block for the next seven years. The 1962 engine line would be continued unchanged for the new 1963 model. The same would be done for the 1967–68 and 1982–84 changeovers, though not for the 1996–97—but that was a long way into the future. The cylinder bore was increased by 1/8 inch to 4 inches and that 4-inch bore was destined to continue in the cast iron small block to the end of 1996 production, a run of 34 years. The throw of the crankshaft was increased so that the stroke lengthened to 3 inches. A good 327 is the most delightful of small blocks, arguably smoother and more willing to rev than the longer stroke 350 cubic inch that followed in 1969.

The range of optional engines was reduced to three, dual carbs were gone and the standard engine had 250 horsepower, 20 more than the 1961 engine, the greater swept volume helping to push the compression ratio up to 10.5:1. The fuelie engine was now rated at 360 horsepower, the most powerful Corvette motor yet.

Above: The beautiful instrument cluster, essentially unchanged since 1958, grouped all the gauges in front of the driver with the tachometer at the center.

33

SPECIFICATIONS

Wheel-base 98"
Length 14' 8"
Width 5' 10"
Weight 3035 lbs
Transmission 2 speed auto
or 3 speed manual
or 4 speed manual
Brakes 11" drum
Engines
  Base 327 V8
  Compression 10.5
  Gross Horse Power 250

  Option L75 327 V8
  Compression 10.5
  Gross Horse Power 300

  Option L76 327 V8
  Compression 11.25
  Gross Horse Power 340

  Option L84 327 V8
    fuel injection
  Compression 11.25
  Gross Horse Power 360

1963

The all-new 1963 Corvette was launched on September 26 1962. The new Chevrolet sports car was astonishing, and finally put to rest the dowdy and dull image of "Economical Transportation," Chevrolet's advertising slogan of the 1930s that had been so carefully nurtured for so long.

The unique shape of the Sting Ray was derived directly from Head of Styling Bill Mitchell's amazing Sting Ray Racer. A total car fanatic of the kind that General Motors has always been too short of, Mitchell lived every moment to the full and wanted a very special Corvette to race. He bought from Chevrolet the chassis of the Mule, one of the two cancelled SS racing cars that had made a brief appearance at the 1957 Sebring 12 hours. Larry Shinoda worked with him to design and have built, with unofficial and unauthorized assistance from GM, his own circuit racer, which they named the Sting Ray. With its airplane-wing cross section, the design was aerodynamically flawed, suffering from obvious front-end lift once the driver exceeded 120mph, but automobile airflow was a little-understood science back then, and the Racer was cleverly developed into the production car.

It is well documented that the new Sting Ray was designed initially as a coupe, and that there was some reluctance among the design team to develop a convertible version of their fabulous new design. Stylists love pure forms and the Aero-Coupe was perfection itself. The aggressive and uncompromising twin back windows emphasized the double curvature of the roof, imagery borrowed from military aircraft of the time, and the

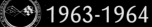

sparkling gas lid with its twin crossed flags left no doubt that it was a Corvette receding into the distance.

There was a bold wind-split motif that started at the front of the roof and then accented the division of the rear fastback window, finishing at the vee where the coupe roof gathered. At one stage an opening rear hatch was proposed, but modern enthusiasts can be grateful that this was abandoned, probably due to cost, because we can envisage the shut lines breaking the form of the tail, the water leaks and the squeaks. As built it was superbly rigid and weatherproof.

The styling staff may have been in love with their Aero-Coupe, but Chevrolet knew that they needed a convertible. After all, open-roof cars had sold successfully for most of the previous ten years and they would not cut a model that worked. They were right, and the convertible would be outselling the coupe two to one within two years. It is easier to make a successful convertible out of a coupe than the other way about and this time it worked perfectly. The soft top had to look right three ways: top up, top down and hardtop on. When open, the Sting Ray's soft top was concealed under a rear-hinged and counterbalanced decklid, just as it had been since the Motorama Corvette of 1953. Power operation, an option of diminishing popularity since 1956, was now abandoned. The top was small and it was quick to raise and lower

Below Top: For 1963 only, conical gauge centers were bright satin finish.

Below Bottom: The headlight pods were swivelled by electric motors.

manually, secured by chrome latches to the windshield header at the front, and by toothed pins into receivers on the rear deck lid.

For 1963, a ladder-type frame replaced the legendary X-frame of the 1953–62. That old frame was immensely strong, the diagonals of the central cruciform and the heavy bolt-in front suspension cross-member very resistant to crash damage and to rust. The new frame was neither as strong nor as rust-resistant, but it allowed the floor pan to be dropped down where appropriate to improve the interior space and the driving position, and swept up at the rear for the all important independent rear suspension. This

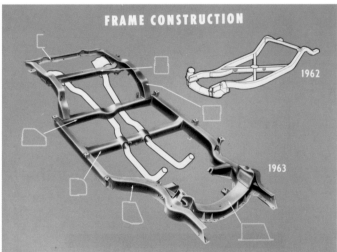

FRAME CONSTRUCTION

1962

1963

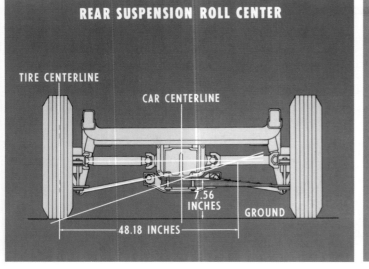

REAR SUSPENSION ROLL CENTER

TIRE CENTERLINE

CAR CENTERLINE

7.56 INCHES

GROUND

48.18 INCHES

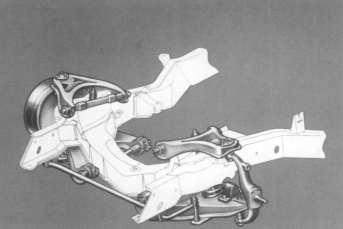

CORVETTE FRONT SUSPENSION

frame remained in production almost unchanged for an amazing twenty years and 660,000 units, and it is remarkable that it should have been so right from the outset.

To make the Corvette an economical proposition as a limited production car from a mass production manufacturer, management had to be convinced that it was using a high content of parts already in use in other model lines. The 1953–62 borrowed the complete front suspension hubs and brakes from the 1949–54 full size Chevrolet, and they were then used for years after the donor car had moved on. The 1963 borrowed less heavily from the corporate parts bin, the base car using only the upper control arms from the 1958–64 full sized car, and the front hubs from the current car too.

A quick steering conversion was ingeniously incorporated into the new model by providing a choice of track rod end holes into the steering arms. The rearmost position was used for the low-geared low-effort position, a standard ratio of 19.6, and the forward for the faster 17.0 ratio, or when the car was fitted with optional power steering—the first time this option had been offered. By 1963 integrated powered steering boxes were available, but the engineers wisely chose steering feel instead, by opting for an outdated system first seen on the classic 1955 Chevrolet passenger car, and about to be superseded. It had a leak-prone control valve, which formed the link between the track arm and a separate ram with four

external hydraulic hoses, but it gave assistance when required, was never intrusive at higher speeds and still allowed the front wheels to communicate road feel to the driver. It looked old fashioned in 1963 but was still being fitted to new Corvettes nineteen years later.

The rear suspension was a revolutionary concept for a Detroit product at the time. Independent rear suspension gives improved traction and improves the ability of the wheel to track over bumps without disturbing the car. It gave the Corvette almost the same geometry as the much more complex Jaguar XKE at a fraction of the cost, still using the drive shaft as the upper link, and a single leaf spring instead of the English manufacturer's four coil springs. Zora Arkus-Duntov went to great lengths to make sure that the new car would handle properly. He had established that a 49/51 front to rear weight distribution would give ideal handling and the new Corvette achieved this. His rear suspension was up to racing car standards of the time, indeed the Corvette had true four-wheel independent suspension before Aston Martin or Ferrari.

In 1963, the new Corvette's fully independent rear suspension had been a sensation, and five years later it was still unique for a domestic car. American engines and transmissions had been superb for years, but the sports car enthusiast had been denied a vehicle that could really put that power to the ground. Show-off kids liked to light up one rear tire, drag racers fitted low pressure slicks to accelerate in a straight line—and lost control if they started

to turn—but here at last was a vehicle in which you could apply full power even on uneven surfaces, and the wheels would just lock to the road and thrust the car forward.

The new 1963 rear suspension was beautifully simple—it had to be, otherwise Chevrolet would have refused to sanction its production on cost grounds alone. It was designed as a three-link system, following principles proven on Zora Arkus-Duntov's wonderful mid-engined CERV-1 experimental hill-climb special and sometime show car. In this car, the drive shaft between the differential and rear wheel spindle was utilized as the top link of the lateral rear suspension parallelogram. This avoided the potentially troublesome splined sleeves that were required when the drive shafts had to vary in length as the suspension moved up and down.

The new Corvette had a much more spacious interior, with larger doors for better access, side windows that could be seen out of without the driver bending and a much more relaxed driving position. The seat was now height-adjustable with a wrench, but a little smaller and narrower. The door armrests looked familiar too, they were the same as were fitted to the previous two year's Corvettes, but the door panels were built to last for years, unlike those of the previous model.

Although the new model was missing a trunk, there was plenty of interior space, particularly in the coupe. If the car was built before the end of March 1963 it had a usefully deep storage recess below each seat. After this date these useful recesses were discontinued, probably because they projected an inch below the transmission cross-member and were being damaged on bad roads.

A new option for the Corvette was air conditioning. Cleverly controlled by just two matching knobs above the clock, flanking the face level outlet, and with neatly installed outlets beneath either end of the dash, this instantly made the Corvette the world's fastest air conditioned production two-seater car. Genuine leather seats were also available for the first time, though the only leather color available that year was Saddle Tan.

The ultimate interior option, available for the coupe only, had to be the 36-gallon fuel tank. Designed for long distance

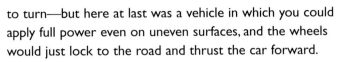

circuit racing, and to improve handling by bringing the weight of the fuel closer to the center of the car, some were sold with cars that had low performance engines or even air conditioning. The tank was made of fiberglass and was installed within the cabin of the coupe. With the optional 3.08:1 Special Highway Axle it could give a fuel range of 700 miles. The original galvanized steel

tank was omitted with option N03, but more than one Southern restorer has reported finding a "big tank" car with the original tank still in place, and a mysterious odor of moonshine coming from the interior-mounted spare tank…

The instrument cluster was perhaps the most striking feature of the 1963 interior. Cast in aluminum, the cluster placed all the instruments boldly in front of the driver. With their cranked orange needles, the deep satin-aluminum conical centers look as though they are turned from solid billet, but in reality they are almost paper-thin pressings of exceptional quality. The lenses were plastic.

To help prevent over-revving of the optional solid lifter-engines, which lacked the self-limiting effect of the hydraulic lifters, a buzzer was installed behind the tachometer, which triggered at 6500rpm. It was discontinued at about the mid-point of production, perhaps because it was not loud enough. The speedometer read to 160mph, and has impressed millions of schoolboys.

The 327 engines were a carryover from 1962, but 1963 was the first year that alternators were fitted to Corvettes—previously dynamos were used on all straight axle models. This change was made right through the General Motors car range for 1963. The advantage of the alternator was that it was capable of powering all lights, the interior fan, windshield wipers and accessories while the engine was at idle speed. It was a beautifully-made and wonderfully reliable unit that would serve until it was replaced by a new design with a solid state internal voltage controller in 1969.

In 1963 the long established Wonderbar AM signal-seeking radio was adapted to fit the vertical format of the space available in the console, and was offered as an option. As well as the normal volume, tuning and preset knobs, this radio had a left-hand automatic tuning bar, which, when pressed, unlatched the tuned station and moved to the next in the pre-selected sensitivity range. The dial had Conelrad markings at 640 and 1240 mhz. This was the height of the Cold War and, in the event of an Emergency, commercial stations would close down and direct listeners to these Civilian Defense frequencies. FM (frequency modulation) radio stations were increasing by 1963 and an AM/FM receiver was offered as option U69 from about March 1963.

The Sting Ray Racer on which the new model was based had no head lamps, and so as not to compromise the beautiful shape concealed headlamps were incorporated. Commonplace today, they were a sensation in September 1962. They were the first hidden headlamps on any car since the pre-war Cord that any one could remember—the 1942 De Soto and Dodge are best forgotten—and the first motorized concealed headlamps on any production car. They were designed for long service with self-aligning ball pivots and gear reduction motors. Thankfully for those of us who love to drive these cars by night thirty-five years after production finished, GM thoughtfully provided manual turn-wheels to override failed motors.

SPECIFICATIONS

Wheel-base 98"
Length 14' 8"
Width 5' 10"
Weight 3110 lbs
Transmission 2 speed auto
  or 3 speed manual
  or 4 speed manual
Brakes 11" drum
Engines
  Base 327 V8
  Compression 10.5
  Gross Horse Power 250

  Option L75 327 V8
  Compression 10.5
  Gross Horse Power 300

  Option L76 327 V8
  Compression 11.25
  Gross Horse Power 365

  Option L84 327 V8
    fuel injection
  Compression 11.25
  Gross Horse Power 375

1964

Changes for 1964 were few. Externally the Coupe lost some brightwork around the windshield, so that the A-pillar was now painted, and the center bar of its rear window—victory of a sort for Arkus-Duntov over Mitchell. The engineer felt that the dividing bar left a blind spot in the center of the rear view mirror, which could hide a motorcycle cop, while styling chief Mitchell quite rightly felt that it was a styling tour de force. They could have compromised by moving the rear view mirror lightly to the right… To help ventilation of the coupe, two air vents and a three-speed extract fan were incorporated in the coupe's B-pillars.

The 1964 hood panel lost its bright metal inserts, the hubcaps were changed, as they would for each year of the C2 shape, and the new Kelsey Hayes aluminum knock-off wheels promised for 1963 appeared at last as a $322.80

option. They looked great, but because of the adapter needed to secure the knock-off wheel to the five-stud hub, they weighed more than the steel wheel and stainless wheel trim. Considerable care was need to keep them secure and modern reproductions have a roll pin lock incorporated to prevent the spinner from loosening.

Engines were a continuation of the 1963 line-up, with more power for the two solid lifter engines thanks to breathing improvements. The optional 4-speed transmission, selected by the majority of buyers, was changed from the Borg-Warner T-10 to GM's own new Muncie, built in the Indiana city of the same name. This came with a more substantial shifter with an attractive fat chrome knob. Inside the car, the door pull knobs were also now chrome, but the centers of the gauges became matt black.

Right: Period GM pictures distinguish between 1963 and 1964 Coupes.

Below: The 1963-1967 Aero Coupe was always outsold by the open top version.

Right: When the White or Silver interior was ordered for 1964, dash, carpet and seats were supplied in another color. Dual color interiors were also available in 1965. The radio, shifter and 1965 teak steering wheel are incorrect in this car.

Below: The rocker panels below doors were different for each year of 1963–67.

Wheel-base 98"
Length 14' 8"
Width 5' 10"
Weight 3145 lbs
Transmission 2 speed auto
 or 3 speed manual
 or 4 speed manual
Brakes 11.75 disc
Engines
 Base 327 V8
 Compression 10.5
 Gross Horse Power 250

 Option L75 327 V8
 Compression 10.5
 Gross Horse Power 300

 Option L79 327 V8
 Compression 11.0
 Gross Horse Power 350

 Option L76 327 V8
 Compression 11.25
 Gross Horse Power 365

 Option L84 327 V8
 fuel injection
 Compression 11.25
 Gross Horse Power 375

 Option L78 396 V8
 Compression 11.0
 Gross Horse Power 425

1965

By 1965 the Corvette was starting to appeal to two quite different kinds of buyers. One group was the influential and ever more European-minded magazine testers, and therefore their readers, who wanted great brakes, taut handling, high revving engines and Jaguar cockpits. The other group was the Main Street enthusiasts, who demanded chrome, straight line acceleration and therefore more cubic inches. Luckily, in 1965 they both got their way.

From the front, the 1965 looked cleaner and stronger, thanks to a new and less fussy black grille with a full bright surround, bigger 7.75 x 15 tires and a plain and unadorned hood panel. A larger pair of crossed flags formed the new nose emblem. From the side the new wheel covers aped the "magnesium" wheels that were starting to become popular, an effect achieved with charcoal paint around the six openings. New rocker trims, plain polished aluminum with a single black recess, contrasted with the bold new

triple vertical vents behind each front wheel. These openings were now active and helped to vent the under-hood area, which would be getting the most powerful base and optional motors yet.

By far the most dramatic externally-fitted option was the new Side Mounted Exhaust. Replacing the rocker moldings below the doors, it lent the Corvette a bad boy image, which did wonders for its credibility. They were cleverly designed to minimize surface heat by introducing an air space between the pipe and the insulated cover. The cover was attractively slotted too, to circulate cooling air—it was claimed that the covers got no hotter than a car body on a hot day in Arizona. They were certainly much cooler and therefore safer than the after-market side pipes that were soon being sold. With their outlets angled down at 45 degrees, they could blow up impressive clouds of dust, sufficient to infuriate neighbors at a

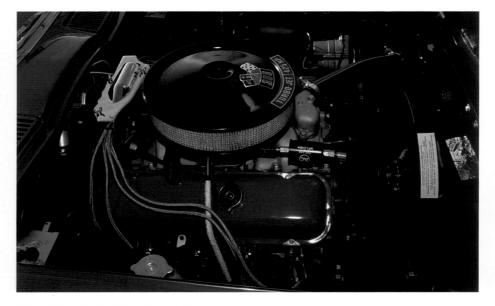

Above: The 425 hp 396 cubic inch big block required a special hood.

Corvette Concours, or to score a point in a Porsche Park. Splitting the banks of cylinders so that the driver heard mainly 1,3,5 and 7 side pipes could sometimes sound like a permanent misfire, but a reassuring dab of the right foot would confirm that all eight were still there. At low revs the engine was tolerably quiet, but once the right pedal was pressed hard the sound "broke through" and the noise was truly glorious. Such was the torque of the engine that one could easily pull away from a stop sign in front of an observing officer without him reaching for his notebook or whistle, and then bid him farewell with powerful blast from a safe distance.

Inside, the seats were improved with fatter and more comfortable construction, and there were bold new door panels too, subtly scooped and sculpted with an integral armrest, the shapes accented by polished stainless steel trims. They looked beautiful but they heralded a new "dark age" in door panel design that would blight the Corvette and other GM cars for an unlucky thirteen years. The

technology was impressive but flawed, for behind the molded vinyl and the polyurethane foam lay humble pressed cellulose pulp board. This soon absorbed the moisture from the outer door area, and within a few years the panel was curling and pulling away from the door. Luckily, during the 1980s enterprising aftermarket vendors recognized the problem and tooled up to make panels with a stiff polypropylene backing instead of pressed pulp, which solved the problem for those with a few hundred dollars to spare. To close the door, a molded self-colored plastic handle with a thin steel inner reinforcement retained by two thin screws was provided, and this too inevitably failed soon. A better solution was found for 1966 with a chromed metal handle, but incredibly the meager 1965 door pull was revived for a further nine years use in the 1969–1977 Corvettes, where it was just as unsatisfactory!

One-piece, press-molded carpet was introduced from 1965, replacing all the bound edges of the previous two years, and neatly fitting into the footwells and around the rear arches. The instruments were also all changed, so that instead of the stylized deep cone faces and cranked instrument needles, the gauges were now had plain black faced dials. A new optional telescopic column was also offered, with a 3-inch adjustment by a six-eared ring below the horn ring.

The 425 horsepower 396 cubic inch big block would be the big surprise for 1965, propelling the Corvette fitted with option L78 to the front of the Muscle Car pack, but this engine was not seen until mid March 1965. The new model range was launched with the four engines carried over from 1964 with minimal changes, and an additional optional engine, the small block RPO L79 327/350. By combining a new hydraulic lifter cam with the 365

horsepower's big valves, 11.0:1 forged pistons and a 4150 Holley carburetor, the engineers made a lively but burst-proof engine, without the mechanical lifter rattles and service requirements of the 365.

The base 250 horsepower, L75 300 hp, L76 solid lifter 365 hp, and L84 fuel injection, continued as for 1964. Unfortunately, this would be the last year for the Rochester fuel injection. It cost almost twice as much the new 425 hp 396, and on paper looked like an expensive way to buy 50 less horsepower. With only 771 units sold in 1965, and a continuing but unjustified reputation for unreliability, it had no hope of survival. But running right, low-miles original or fully restored, there are few American engines made in the last 33 years that can offer such a stunning reaction to a jab on the right pedal.

The new big block was quickly nicknamed the Porcupine because of the multi-directional disposition of its valves. These used ball-mounted rockers like the small block's, but the studs and valves were cleverly angled to allow a "semi-hemi" combustion chamber, which could accommodate massive 2.19 inch intake and 1.72 inch exhaust valves, and better shaped inlet and exhaust ports. The cylinder heads gave an 11.0:1 compression ratio and power output was an impressive 425hp.

By far the most significant innovation on the 1965 Corvette was the change to four-wheel disc brakes that were a revelation. Not just incredibly powerful, and capable of repeated stops from high speed, they were beautifully progressive too. They were designed to the very best standards of the time and without any compromise on performance. To spread the load on the large friction pads equally, the caliper had four pistons, two each side, and was rigidly mounted. By contrast, today's

Left: Wheel covers changed every year, aluminum wheels were an option.

cars calipers usually have pistons on one side only and an often troublesome sliding mount to compensate. The discs were fully ventilated, 1-1/4 inch thick and 11-1/2 inch diameter and vacuum power boost was optional. The calipers were not designed with a parking brake in mind, so a small, separate, cable-operated, drum-type brake was built into the center offset of the rear rotor.

Long term, and mainly through lack of maintenance, the calipers and parking brake were both terribly troublesome. If the fluid in the brake system was changed regularly—preferably annually—then the calipers would last indefinitely. But brake fluid is hygroscopic—that is it absorbs water vapor from the atmosphere—and this water would

condense in the calipers and cause the polished cast iron bores to rust. Once the bores were pitted, no amount of re-sealing, cleaning or polishing would restore the seal.

Happily, the stainless-steel-sleeved exchange caliper was invented in about 1976, offering a cheap and reliable replacement. Hidden away inside the rotor, well away from regular maintenance, the parking or emergency brake also deteriorated fast. The operating levers rusted together and relied on a slot in the thin dust shield for location. Again stainless steel mechanisms have effectively solved this problem, but if the 6.5-inch diameter drums of the emergency brake were relied on to stop the car, then a real emergency would surely follow!

Right: Flip up headlights have been a Corvette trade mark since 1963.

Left: The Corvette body is retained to the frame by just 8 bolts. A restored rolling chassis looks so great that it can be hard to put the body back on!

SPECIFICATIONS

Wheel-base 98"
Length 14' 8"
Width 5' 10"
Weight 3145 lbs
Transmission 2 speed auto
    or 3 speed manual
    or 4 speed manual
Brakes 11.75 disc
Engines
    Base 327 V8
    Compression 10.5
    Gross Horse Power 300

    Option L79 327 V8
    Compression 11.0
    Gross Horse Power 350

    Option L36 427 V8
    Compression 10.25
    Gross Horse Power 390

    Option L72 427 V8
    Compression 11.00
    Gross Horse Power 425

1966

1966 would be a golden year for the Sting Ray. Sales reached an all time high of 27,720, almost double the boom year of 1962, and for the Chevrolet Division the investment in advanced engineering and styling had paid off handsomely. A radical restyling of the body on the same chassis had been developed and was being readied for production. Strong sales of the 1966 would ensure that the project would be successful.

The engine option list was culled from five to three, out went the sweet mannered 250 horsepower 327, and its raucous mechanical lifter brothers, the carbureted 365 hp and the fuel injected 375. In came another big block, the 390 horsepower L36. This was the prime time of the muscle car era, and the Corvette had the engines to deliver. By the end of the year more than a third of sales would have been big blocks.

The traditional convertible was holding up too, with open car sales heading towards two thirds of total production. Only five years previously many of the Styling Staff had wanted the Corvette to be a coupe only.

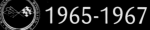

The external changes for 1966 model year were minor compared to the previous two. Viewed from the front, a one-piece die-cast grille replaced the sometimes frail designs of previous years. New Corvette Sting Ray emblems, with the Corvette script now standing vertical, replaced the italic version used since 1963. For the first and only time this script appeared on the front driver's side of the hood panel, as well as on the rear panel.

From the side, there was the inevitable change to the rocker panel, which returned to a fluted design reminiscent of the 1963. As with the 1965, this panel was omitted if side pipes were specified, and a narrow rocker

trim replaced it, the same unit used through 1967. The grilles on the roof pillars were discarded because the interior stale air exhaust system was now discontinued, and the B-pillars were now completely smooth.

Similar in shape to those of 1965, the seats were treated to large panels with transverse pleats—only the 1959 Corvette had previously had pleats across the car. New too for 1966 were optional "Strato-ease" headrests. There was increasing awareness of auto safety in the mid-sixties, and in particular of whiplash injuries caused to the occupants of a vehicle hit from the rear, which were reduced when head rests were fitted. A major improvement was the

49

relocation of the parking brake to between the seats. This gave better leverage and the cable distance was shorter, but the brake would still struggle to stop the loaded car.

The newcomer engine for 1966 was another big block, the L36 390 hp 427, the biggest yet in a Corvette. Asked why the engineers had at last breached the self-imposed Corporate 400 cubic inch capacity and introduced a 427, Zora Arkus-Duntov was reported to have replied that it was purely a weight saving measure, boring out the block to 4.25 inches saved a lot of iron! Breathing through a 4160 Holley, this engine delivered a staggering 460 lb.ft. at only 3600rpm. With this much torque, the car was truly remarkable to drive. It was as easy to set off in third gear as in first, there was often no need to downshift to pass, and if you liked a little wheel spin it was there for the taking. Tried on a familiar hilly road, the sheer torque meant that when you would normally be ready to shift in third or second, you would realize that there was no need to shift at all. The 390 horsepower would flatten hills.

Above: The L-79 327-350 hp small block.

Below: 1966 was the last year for optional knock-off aluminum wheels. This 427 big block also has the loud side exhaust option.

Maryland

503 OOL

Historic

Left: The coupe had cutaway roof for easier access.

Above: Back-up lights were standard equipment from 1966.

SPECIFICATIONS

Wheel-base 98"
Length 14' 8"
Width 5' 10"
Weight 3145 lbs
Transmission 2 speed auto
   or 3 speed manual
   or 4 speed manual
Brakes 11.75 disc
Engines
  Base 327 V8
  Compression 10.5
  Gross Horse Power 300

  Option L79 327 V8
  Compression 11.0
  Gross Horse Power 350

  Option L36 427 V8
  Compression 10.25
  Gross Horse Power 390

  Option L68 427 V8
  Compression 10.25
  Gross Horse Power 400

  Option L71 427 V8
  Compression 11.0
  Gross Horse Power 435

  Option L88 427 V8
  Compression 12.5
  Gross Horse Power 430
   (probably true 550)

1967

1967 was the last year of production for the Sting Ray. It was replaced by the 1968 Corvette, which had no fishy name, and then the name came back as one word—Stingray—in 1969. It is likely that the 1967 was originally intended to be the shark nosed car, but that delays with the design caused its postponement for a year.

Faced with modernizing the Sting Ray one more time, the Styling Staff gave it a makeover that reflected the value and now maturity of the concept, cutting back on the glitter and letting the beautiful body shape speak for itself. The most obvious change was the new and wider Rally wheels, replacing at last the succession of tinny hubcaps that had adorned base model Corvettes for so long. The wider rims helped to fill out the wheel openings and made the car appear more assured. Behind each front wheel a new five-louvered grille leaned forward with italic urgency,

Above Left: 1967 327 small block 4 barrel Holley.

Above Middle: 1967 427 big block with triple two barrel Holleys.

Left: Side exhausts were available only from 1965 to 1967.

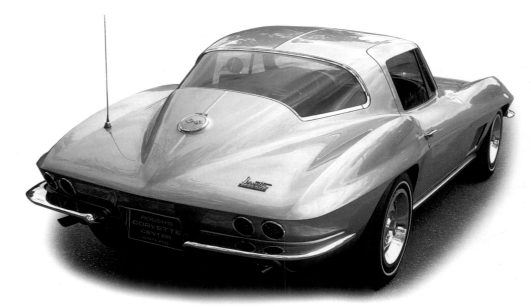

Above Right: The L-88 427 big block, probably 550 horsepower.

Left: The black vinyl covering was available for the optional hard-top in 1967 only

and for the first time there was no side emblem at all to break the flow of the fender. At the front, the nose emblem had shrunk and there was no script on the hood, while at the rear the gas lid used none of the usual clear plastic, nor gold paint, just a small crossed flag on plain body color with a thin chrome surround. The whole car was now more graceful and conservative.

With the 1967 427 the designers let their imaginations go, and came up with an outstanding hood with contrasting colored panel, that proclaimed the glory of the five optional big blocks that it could cover, and still avoided an emblem on the front fender. The color of the hood stripe related to, but did not always match, the interior color. The optional Quick take-off wheel was now replaced by the conventionally-mounted N89 bolt-on aluminum wheel. A superb update of the appealing 1966 wheel, the spinner of which was now said to be prohibited by Federal mandate for safety reasons, was replaced by a starburst cover, which required a screwdriver for removal.

A new 400 horsepower L68 engine now joined the big block line up. This combined the basic specification of the 390 with a new concept, for Corvette, of a triple two-barrel carburetor set up. It offered a 10 horsepower improvement over the L36 at 5400rpm, while the all-important torque figure remained unchanged. The 3 x 2 system was capable of flowing 1000 cubic feet per minute, and was promoted as offering improved fuel economy. On this Chevrolet/Holley system the two outer, or secondary, throttle plates were opened solely by diaphragms sensing venturi vacuum at the center or primary carburetor. The throttle linkage could only close, not open the outer throttle plates.

There were two more big block options for the brave in 1967. An original of either today is extremely valuable, and a fake all too easy to build. Selecting option L89 put cast 3904392 aluminum heads onto an L71, converting it into an L89 car. Only 16 of these were sold. The weight saving was impressive, the opportunity for deceit today even more so. The number of owners who think they own an L89 certainly exceeds the number built by Chevrolet.

Bringing the total number of optional engines to a new high of six was the L88. This was a motor built to offer the ultimate in big block performance. It was built for the track and based broadly on the L71. The carburetor was a monster Holley R3418A atop a cast aluminum intake manifold. The compression ratio was 12.5:1, specified idle speed was 1000rpm and the fuel had minimum 103 research octane. No pollution control equipment was fitted, induction was through a special cold air hood, which took high-pressure air from the windshield base, and filtered it through a hood-mounted filter. A special race-only, side-mounted exhaust was offered and other heavy-duty options were required. Only twenty were built and Chevrolet avoided mentioning a horsepower figure—it was probably in excess of 550.

SPECIFICATIONS

Wheel-base 98"
Length 14' 11"
Width 5' 10"
Weight 3220 lbs
Transmission 3 speed auto
   or 3 speed manual
   or 4 speed manual
Brakes 11.75 disc
Engines
  Base 327 V8
  Compression 10.5
  Gross Horse Power 300

  Option L79 327 V8
  Compression 11.0
  Gross Horse Power 350

  Option L36 427 V8
  Compression 10.25
  Gross Horse Power 390

  Option L68 427 V8
  Compression 10.25
  Gross Horse Power 400

  Option L71 427 V8
  Compression 11.0
  Gross Horse Power 435

  Option L89 427 V8
  Compression 11.0
  Gross Horse Power 435

  Option L88 427 V8
  Compression 12.5
  Gross Horse Power 430
   (probably true 550)

1968

Thirty-five years after its September 1967 launch, the 1968 Corvette is still one of the most sensational shapes ever devised for a production car. It was a triumph for Bill Mitchell's GM Styling Staff and Larry Shinoda, who had been involved with Mitchell's Corvette projects since the days of the Sting Ray Racer and was largely responsible for the 63–67 Corvette styling too.

The all-new body of the 1968 was fitted to the same chassis that had been used for the five previous years. Indeed, with just a few days' work it is quite possible to interchange the bodies of a 1967 and a 1968. The T-roof coupe was a first for Chevrolet—combining a removable back window, it gave all the fresh air and freedom of the convertible with the roll-over protection of the coupe. The rear window fitted beneath the rear deck in its own swing-down compartment. The convertible had outsold the coupe by almost two to one over the previous five years of the

Sting Ray era and the trend continued for 1968, helped perhaps by a $343 price advantage to the convertible.

The exterior of the new Corvette was stunning, but the steeply-raked windshield, low roof, sloped door glass and pinched coke bottle waistline all meant that the interior was going to be tight. No problem with that in a sports car perhaps, but the seat had to be raked back further than in the previous model, 33 degrees instead of 25, and shoulder room was tight.

Molded vinyl with injected polyurethane foam was used first for the door panels in 1965 and did not wear well. The early 1968 door panel was particularly unsatisfactory, with no proper internal door pull—only a horizontal hand slot which soon fell apart, later corrected with a separate horizontal handle. The standard seats were finished in a coarse "basket weave" vinyl. Leather was an option, and carpets were loop material. In contrast to the 1963–67

Left: The shape of the new 1968 was a sensation, bystanders would ask new owners "Where are the wipers?"

Above: The Targa roof coupe was a new feature for 1968, became a Corvette tradition and started the trend away from convertibles.

Right: The chromed rack was a popular option, always fitted by the dealer, not the factory. Back-up lamps were hidden beneath the rear bumpers.

Left: Base engine was this 300 hp 327. The vacuum canister at left of picture lifts the wiper flap.

instrument cluster, the big-diameter 160mph speedo and 7000 rpm tach were recessed deep into a sculpted panel of vinyl-faced, impact-absorbing polyurethane foam. The ignition switch position at the top right hand of the dash, beside the tachometer, was unique to the 1968. The steering wheel was 16-inch diameter and similar, though not interchangeable with the previous four years' wheel. An optional telescopic column was selected by less than a quarter of buyers.

Nominally a carryover from 1967, the 1968 327 shared almost no part numbers with its predecessor—indeed the crankshaft was unique to Corvette in 1968 and will interchange with no other model year. This has meant that a correct 1968 Corvette small block is a tough engine for the restorer to find. The 1968 327 was a transitional engine, caught on the cusp between the rev hungry 327, whose architecture dated back to the 1955 265, and the emissions-ready 350, which would power the Corvette through the mid-1990s. Previous 327s had solid valve covers, an oil filler pipe that fitted into the front of half of the intake manifold, and—most importantly—a crankcase vent at the back of the block just beside the distributor. For the 350, which followed in 1969, Chevrolet decided to sacrifice appearance for efficiency and some cost savings, and arranged for all crank case ventilation and oil filling to be via the valve covers. The 1968 327 was transitional, because while it had the crankcase ventilation via the valve

Right: The "Futuristic" option P01 full wheel cover was a popular option in 1968, only this year had 7" width wheel rims.

Left: This early 1968 has the forward mounted external rear view mirror. It was positioned further back during the production run. The secondary door release knob was hard to use and changed for the following year.

covers in the style of the new generation 350, the oil filler was still in the front of the intake manifold.

All 1968 Corvettes were built with an air injection reactor (AIR) system installed, even the race-only L88. This was belt-driven, and forced fresh air into the exhaust manifolds to promote a secondary burn of the combustion gases in the exhaust system, and thus reduce emission of unburned hydrocarbon. Undoubtedly the ugliest engine accessory ever devised, the pump and its associated plumbing and valves were discarded wholesale by enthusiastic owners, this one included. For originality, the whole system should be in place.

For 1968 two previously alien systems were introduced, fiber optics for external lamp monitoring and vacuum for control of heating, ventilation, air conditioning and external moving surfaces. If that sounds like something from the airplane industry, then the stylists succeeded in their aims. Undoubtedly, they would like to have had a vacuum-controlled rear spoiler and vacuum-operated flip up brake lights too, but we must be forever grateful that we got the moving surfaces we did. The flip-up headlamps work reliably and well, powered by big reversible vacuum actuators, which in turn were controlled by vacuum relays. The otherwise conventional windshield wipers and washer system were cleverly hidden by a lifting flap. Pushing the console-mounted switch signaled the vacuum actuator to raise the flap, which in turn allowed the wipers to start. Switching off the engine triggered an impressive shutdown

Right: Black vinyl covering was optional on all 1968-1975 hard tops.

Left: The special cold air induction hood of this 427 shows that it must be an L88. Chevrolet quoted a diplomatic 430 horsepower, we now know that the true figure was about 550!

sequence. A fiber optic lamp monitor system checked all the external lighting, except back-up and side markers, linking small lenses in the reflector of each lamp to displays at the front and rear of the shift console.

The 1968 Corvette was the first to be fitted with a three-speed Turbo Hydra-Matic 400 automatic transmission, first used in other Chevrolets in 1965. This was a serious heavy-duty unit, widely regarded as one of the best and used in a wide range of vehicles from trucks to Rolls Royces and Jaguars.

The new-look slotted Kelsey Hayes Rally Wheel was continued from the 1967 Sting Ray, but was widened to 7 inches for 1968 and fitted with larger centercap and outer trims. The new Bright Metal Wheel Cover, costing an extra $57.95 for the set, was quite different to anything previously offered, a futuristic vision with 72 fins radiating from a cross-flagged center emblem. It marked a wheel design direction that no one else would follow, but was ordered by more than 30% of 1968 buyers. Wider wheels meant wider tires, and the base tire for 1968 was a blackwall F70x15 bias-ply nylon cord. Whitewall tires were gone on Corvettes, now it was the age of the stripe tire— narrow white or narrow red stripe. To drive a car on bias belt nylon tires today is a memorable experience, because the ride, steering feel and wet traction is so incredibly bad. Original or not, these are high performance cars and need modern radial tires.

Chevrolet had been hard at work developing and refining their unique fiberglass sports car, because by 1969—from any angle—its stance was improved. It looked wider, more confident and even more aggressive than the previous year's model. This improved appearance was due to the new wider 8-inch Rally wheels. In three successive production years the wheel size had increased annually by an inch, and now the wheels really filled the arches. Tire size remained unchanged, with the same F 70 15 belted tires as the 1968, but stretching them onto the wider rim

emphasized the fatness of the "70" profile, then the lowest profile that could be bought. These really showed off the white or red stripes factory-fitted for the majority of buyers.

Behind the front wheels, chromed die-cast trims could be now be ordered to emphasize the four vents. First seen as a 1965 option and much missed in 1968, this loud side exhaust was something that no other mass-produced car offered as a factory option.

The front fenders were adorned with new chrome-plated metal Stingray emblems in italic script. Now Corvettes could once again be called by an alternate name, and owners of 1968s were quick to update their cars too. At the rear, the 1969 model lost its back-up lights, these were now incorporated with red reflectors into the space previously occupied by the inner pair of rear lamps. So now it was harder to spot those Corvettes at night again, which probably saved a few tickets from being issued too.

A first for an American production car, the headlights were now fitted with washers that were teed off the main washer system and washed the outer of the pairs of lamps whenever the windshield washer button was pressed. While this emptied the small washer bottle twice as quickly as before and was an impressive talking point, it was quietly dropped within two years, never to be seen again on a Corvette.

Left: Giant big block valve covers were chrome plated only in 1968 and 1969. All big block engines were built at the Tonowanda, New York engine plant.

SPECIFICATIONS

Wheel-base 98"
Length 14' 11"
Width 5' 10"
Weight 3245 lbs
Transmission 3 speed auto
 or 3 speed manual
 or 4 speed manual
Brakes 11.75 disc
Engines
 Base 350 V8
 Compression 10.25
 Gross Horse Power 300

 Option L46 350 V8
 Compression 11.0
 Gross Horse Power 350

 Option L36 427 V8
 Compression 10.25
 Gross Horse Power 390

 Option L68 427 V8
 Compression 10.25
 Gross Horse Power 400

 Option L71 427 V8
 Compression 11.0
 Gross Horse Power 435

 Option L89 427 V8
 Compression 11.0
 Gross Horse Power 435

 Option L88 427 V8
 Compression 12.5
 Gross Horse Power 430
 (probably true 550)

1969

For 1969 there were many improvements. The outside door handles were simplified and easier to use, because the protruding push-knob needed to open the 1968 door was gone, replaced by a mechanism neatly incorporated into the upper door handle flap.

Above: L-68 427 cubic inch 400 hp big block with triple Holley 2 barrel carburettors.

A smaller, black-rimmed, 15-inch diameter steering wheel replaced the 16-inch simulated wood grain wheel of the 1968. A new optional tilt and telescopic steering column and restyled door panels made the 1969 interior much more appealing for the driver. There were more than 40 Corvette options in 1969, the most ever, if the convertible body is considered an option and color choices are ignored. This does not mean that the cars would be any less well equipped in the future, just that many of the options would become standard.

The convertible body effectively became an option in 1969, being outsold by the T-roof coupe. Previously the convertible had always outsold the closed car, but in 1969 the situation quickly reversed and the convertible rapidly lost ground to the coupe. There were many social

Right: Side pipes were a factory option for 1969, but can be fitted to any 1968-82. 1969 included numerous improvements over 1968.

Below: A 427 big block convertible with side pipes is one of the most desirable Corvettes. Fender gill trims were optional, 8" rim Rally wheels would continue as base equipment through 1982.

Right: The 4-speed Muncie transmission had a fat chrome shifter with a black chromed ball. Fiber optic rear lamp monitors are visible behind the shifter.

and cultural changes happening in the United States at that time. Convertible drivers are outgoing and have to look cheerful, but from 1967 to 1969 a more introspective attitude began to prevail and the pale, long-haired and serious driver in considered clothing became the fashion ideal. Such people traveled mysteriously, behind tinted glass and hiding their feelings behind sunglasses. Music was now part of the affluent lifestyle, and the car was turning into an entertainment center. A closed car kept the hair tidy, was quieter at speed and was a secure home for the precious 8-track player and stereo tape cartridges, which were never safe beneath a folding roof.

The most desirable of all Stingray non-engine options was the side mounted exhaust system, only available in 1969. It followed the same principles established on the 1965–67 version, sweeping out behind the front wheel to meet the long oval muffler. A fluted cast aluminum cover with internal insulation hid the muffler and protected the legs of the occupants. They sounded great, but could be tiring on a long drive.

The door panels were changed to allow slightly more interior space, and a color-matched vertical plastic door pull was provided at the front of the door. This pull was exactly the same part as the 1965 plastic door pull, but used in reverse, a part so flimsy that it was replaced in the 1966 Sting Ray by a nice chunky satin chromed pull. Needing a cheap and collapsible handle for the 1969 panel, someone remembered the 1965 unit. The bean counters in the back office must have thrilled at the thought of re-using tooling that had been abandoned after only a year, and this hopeless piece of plastic was revived and fitted to all of the next 300,000 Corvettes made until the end of 1977!

The ignition key and cylinder were moved from the dashboard to a position half-way up the right side of the steering column for 1969. A cable interlock prevented removal of the square-headed ignition key, unless the manual shifter was in reverse or the automatic selector in park, and the gears and steering were then locked.

For the 1969 model year the 350 small block replaced the 327, with 5.7 liters instead of 5.4. This engine size was destined to be powering Corvettes for at least the next 33 years. The extra capacity was achieved by use of a longer 3.48-inch stroke crankshaft in place of the 327's 3.25 inch. Sensibly, the connecting rod length was once again 5.7 inch, the longer stroke being accommodated within the piston, which had a shorter pin-to-crown height on the 350.

1969 was the year of the ZL1. The ZL1 was essentially an L88 with an aluminum block in lieu of cast iron and was fitted with steel liners. The block itself was about 100 pounds lighter than its cast iron sister. It was more powerful than the L88, with figures of up to 580 horsepower suggested. Pistons had big domes and yielded a 12.5:1 compression ratio. The ZL1 Corvette was shown as regular production option RPO ZL1 in Chevrolet's end of year production report, which also stated that two were built. In more than thirty years only one ZL1 has been positively identified as genuine, and at the time of writing the whereabouts of the second car is still an exciting mystery.

Top: 1969 cockpit showing optional tilt and telescopic column with smaller steering wheel.

Right: The L88 hood incorporated a power producing cold air system, feeding high pressure air fresh from below the windshield to a hood mounted air cleaner.

Below: 1969 was the first to use the Stingray name on the fender.

Above: A 550 horsepower 7 liter L88. The hood mounted air cleaner closed onto seal shown.

Left: As well as the T-roofs, the rear window on 1968-1972 was removable and stowed in its own compartment.

SPECIFICATIONS

Wheel-base 98"
Length 14' 11"
Width 5' 10"
Weight 3285 lbs
Transmission 3 speed auto
   or 4 speed manual
Brakes 11.75 disc
Engines
   Base 350 V8
   Compression 10.25
   Gross Horse Power 300

   Option L46 350 V8
   Compression 11.0
   Gross Horse Power 350

   Option LT1 350 V8
   Compression 11.0
   Gross Horse Power 370

   Option LS5 454 V8
   Compression 10.25
   Gross Horse Power 390

1970

For many the 1970 was the beginning of a golden age of Corvette design, an age that ended with the last chrome front bumper in July of 1972. Thereafter the intrusive hand of government would be felt in the design of all cars sold in the United States and the first impact would strike the front bumper of the 1973. 1970–1972 Corvettes generally feel and drive better than 1969s, which in turn are almost always better than 1968s. While they are essentially the same cars, there were many minor detailed improvements that, along with the better seats, make them more satisfying to drive.

Perhaps knowing that they were even then enjoying the last days of aggressive front end metalwork, the stylists removed the cheap plastic grilles, utilitarian parking lamps and separate lower moldings and replaced them with a magnificent pair of chromed, die-cast grilles, which incorporated both the lower trims and shapely new parking lamps. The grille was a masterly demonstration of what Detroit then did so well, a superb casting in which the multiple square grille apertures were finished in satin gray, emphasizing the bright finish on the front.

The parking lamp lenses were clear plastic with an amber bulb, but in 1972 the lens material was changed to amber and a clear bulb was used instead. The side marker lamps increased in size and were now set flush with the body. The rear marker lamps were larger too, and both had die-cast metal bodies. The four-wheel openings were given extensions to act as mud deflectors; the 8-inch wheels of the 1969 had thrown up more road dirt than the previous 7-inch wheels, so it was logical do something about the "rooster tails" of mud on the sides of the car. This was an all-weather car with non-rusting bodywork, and there was no reason to leave it at home when the roads were wet. The extensions didn't keep the sides of the car clean, but lowered the tide mark.

The most obvious and effective change to the body was the new front fender air vents, which were given new cast outlet grilles in the style of the front intakes, giving a more horizontal and sleek emphasis to the side of the car. They were painted body color, with the chromed pattern subtly exposed. On cars up to the first few weeks of 1971 production, the chrome was exposed only on the horizontals.

Between the wheels, the two-piece fiberglass and aluminum rocker molding assembly was replaced by a single aluminum trim, covering the otherwise exposed frame side rail. This part, like so many on the Stingray, was destined for another 12 years of service. The dramatic side exhaust had been discontinued at the end of the 1969 model year, although it could still be bought and fitted as an over-the-counter part and can be fitted to any C3, where local legislation permits. To compensate for the lack of a side exhaust option for 1970, two great-looking new rectangular rear exhaust outlets emphasized the power and purpose of the car. They were made of chrome-plated steel, framed in turn by chromed die-cast bezels.

Other changes were more subtle. All cars now had tinted glass. The new 1970 colors were much improved, while Black, a staple almost every year since 1954, was

There were many improvements for 1970, including:

Opposite Top Left: Improved seats.

Opposite Top Right: New cast fender grille.

Right: Rectangular exhaust outlets.

unavailable and would not reappear for another seven years; these were times for subtle metallic shades. Though no figures are available for colors for 1969 or 1970, we know that in both 1968 and 1971 the most popular colors were British Green and Brands Hatch Green respectively. Surprisingly too, Red was never the most popular color for any of the years 1968–1982. Indeed, the most popular color for the all the C3 production, by a big margin, is technically not a color at all—white!

The big block hood and painted hood striping and decals were used for the new 370 horsepower LT1. The striping was spray painted using a disposable mask and the stripes were notoriously uneven. The stripes were black on White, Silver, Yellow and Orange cars, and white on the remainder.

New seats were taller and better shaped, with no separate headrest. The backrest release was moved to the top back of the seat, so hinging the seat-back forward to load the luggage area was now a single-handed task. A shoulder level trim piece accommodated the shoulder belt, standard on coupes and optional on the convertible. The door panels were revised and slimmed again, and finished with a deep metal trim along the middle of the panel. Loop carpet was used with the base trim. Custom Interior Trim now replaced the previous two years' Genuine Leather Seats. This brought with it leather seats and more luxurious cut pile carpet, but was only available in Black or Saddle. The stitched panels of the leather seats for 1970 and half of 1971 were longitudinal, like the vinyl seats, but changed to across the car for the rest of the

Above Right: Both optional 350 small blocks had finned aluminum valve covers. Polished shielding limited radio interference from the ignition wires.

this period and through 1974 too. Today, vendors offer the full of range colors in leather and it is hard indeed to restore, say, a 1972 red interior, and not give oneself leather to sit on.

1970 was almost the last year for unbridled horsepower until the electronic-fuel-injection-led revival of the mid-Eighties, and there were changes to all but the base 300 horsepower engine. The new rev-hungry, solid lifter LT1, originally destined for 1969 production and proven that year in the Camaro Z28 in a five liter 302 form, came out a full size 350 for the Corvette, while the big block engine choice was curtailed in range, but expanded to a monster 7.4 liters as the 454.

Above: Wheel openings were changed to incorporate mud deflecting lower flares.

Left: 1970 Corvettes had new die cast nose and fender grilles. Rocker trim was now one piece aluminum.

SPECIFICATIONS

Wheel-base 98"
Length 14' 11"
Width 5' 10"
Weight 3285 lbs
Transmission 3 speed auto
or 4 speed manual
Brakes 11.75 disc
Engines
Base 350 V8
Compression 8.5
Gross Horse Power 270

Option LT1 350 V8
Compression 9.0
Gross Horse Power 330

Option LS5 454 V8
Compression 8.5
Gross Horse Power 365

Option LS6 454 V8
Compression 9.0
Gross Horse Power 425

1971

1971 saw the last of the really wicked big blocks. Just 188 were made of the aluminum-headed hydraulic lifter LS6, which was rated at 425hp. If you find a 1971 LS6, you have hit gold, and if it's a ZR2 then you've struck the mother lode. Only 12 of these very special order Stingrays were in the ZR2 specification, which included a dual plate clutch, M22 rock-crusher 4-speed, dual-pin heavy-duty power brakes, heavy-duty suspension and aluminum radiator. Not permitted were power steering, radio or air conditioning. 1972 was the end of the first performance era, the LS6 was dropped and other engines nominally down-rated to reflect their horsepower as installed with alternators, air cleaners and full exhaust systems connected. Be in no doubt that we are now in the much longer second performance era, and to prove it just put a recent 1990 ZR1 or a 2001 Z06 against the best of 1965 to 1971!

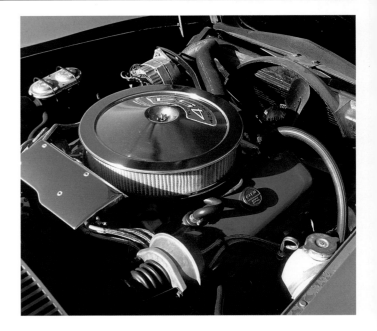

Right: The solid lifter LT-1 used the big block hood with special striping in white or black, depending on paint color.

Above: By 1971 twice as many T-roof coupes were being produced as convertibles. All small blocks except the LT-1 used this plain hood.

Above: From 1970 much improved high back seats were fitted.

SPECIFICATIONS

Wheel-base 98"
Length 14' 11"
Width 5' 10"
Weight 3285 lbs
Transmission 3 speed auto
 or 4 speed manual
Brakes 11.75 disc
Engines
 Base 350 V8
 Compression 8.5
 Net Horse Power 200

 Option LT1 350 V8
 Compression 9.0
 Net Horse Power 255

 Option LS5 454 V8
 Compression 8.5
 Net Horse Power 270

1972

If you are only ever going to own just one big block Corvette, make it a 1970 to 1972 LS5, which in the first year made 500 ft.lbs. of torque at 3,400 rpm. For 1972, that figure was still 390 ft.lbs. even with low compression pistons and an honest, as installed, SAE rating. That is still more torque than the 1993–1995 multi-cam, multi-valve, all-aluminum LT5 developed at 4,800 rpm!

Below: 1972 was the last to have a chromed steel front bumper, thereafter Federal regulations would play an increasing role in the design of the Corvette and all other cars sold in the US.

Above: The standard engine for 1972 was this 200 net hp 350, here with air conditioning and power assisted brakes. Virtually the same engine was rated at a gross 270 hp in 1971.

SPECIFICATIONS

Wheel-base 98"
Length 15' 5"
Width 5' 10"
Weight 3415 lbs
Transmission 3 speed auto
or 4 speed manual
Brakes 11.75 disc
Engines
Base L48 350 V8
Compression 8.5
Net Horse Power 190

Option L82 350 V8
Compression 9.0
Net Horse Power 250

Option LS4 454 V8
Compression 8.5
Net Horse Power 275

1973

The Corvette has succeeded in achieving its 50th birthday because the engineers and stylists have adapted the car when necessary to accommodate changes in taste, driving habits, lifestyle and particularly the 1970's changes in the law. Chevrolet were not scared of spending money not just to update the car to meet the legal requirements, but to actually improve it at the same time. Just how well they could achieve this was shown with the September 1972 launch of the 1973 Corvette.

Faced with the dual challenge of cleaning up the emissions of two different V8 engines and redesigning for an onerous 5 mph barrier test, it would have been easy for Chevrolet to consign the Corvette to the history books after 20 good years. The barrier test required the car to be driven into a solid wall of concrete, and be able to reverse away with all lighting and control systems intact. While European manufacturers tacked heavy-looking separate rubber bumpers onto their US export lines, Chevrolet made a virtue of necessity and extended their long nose design to meet the new regulations for 1973, making it even more attractive.

This was an ingenious and simple solution to the Federal requirements, and went no further than was required by the law. In an impact, the inner metal bumper bar and its support assembly was free to move backward by up to 3½ inches, but was limited by two energy-absorbing bolts, which were reduced in diameter by being drawn through a pair of die nuts. The rival MGB and Jaguar XJS arrived off the boats with black rubber battering rams on their previously elegant fronts, while Chevrolet made their car more elegant. The British engineers looked at the new US bumper regulations and

decided that if the Yanks wanted battering rams then that was what they would jolly well get, but the Corvette represented a triumph of design over expediency.

The new soft nose extended the overall length of the car by just 2.2 inches. Manufactured of a flexible urethane, it would deform in an impact and then revert to its original shape, hopefully shedding not too much of its flexibly formulated paint. Unfortunately heat, and perhaps ultra-violet light, degraded the urethane plastic material, allowing it to go brittle and then crumble, but today's replacements use better plastics technology and are much superior. The front grilles were cast aluminum alloy and, uniquely on the 1973, the leading edge of the grille slats and matching ribs on the clear plastic lamp assembly were accented with silver paint. The optional front license plate bracket could either be fitted in front of the center grille, or replace it to recess the plate between the over riders.

Radial tires at last appeared on the Corvette in 1973. Apparently scared of the effects that fitting radial tires would have on the ride and perceived vibration and harshness in the car, new softer and fatter body mount donuts replaced the previous thin rubber mounts. The body was thus raised an inch, giving useful scope for larger tires in the future. Enthusiasts had been fitting radial tires

to their Corvettes for years, and it was hard to believe that the car's manufacturer had not noticed their many advantages. Virtually all European cars had been fitted with radial tires since the mid 1960s, but they were harder to obtain in the larger size fitted to American cars, and the GR70-15 size which the Corvette needed. Firestone and Goodyear were proudly announced as suppliers for the revolutionary new radials for the 1973 Corvette, and each gave the impression that they alone had perfected this new technology. Firestone launched the Steel Radial 500 and Goodyear the Steelguard. What followed was a debacle for Firestone when the Steel Radial 500 had to be recalled, following numerous instances of thrown tire tread.

The complex concealed windshield wiper system of 1968–72 was abandoned, the wipers now lifting out of a trough behind the flipped up edge of the all-new hood. Now the same for both 350 and 454 engined cars, the

hood was taller and featured a cold air induction system. This ducted cold, and therefore dense, outside air from the pressurized zone at the base of the windshield directly to the air cleaner and carburetor, thus improving the density of the engine's intake air and therefore its performance. Under hard acceleration, a wonderful and moaning roar was heard from this device, which never failed to impress.

For 1973 the base engine, now known as L-48, was rated ten horsepower down on the 1972, at a meager 190hp. This was the first time since the 1955 introduction of the V8 as a 265 cubic engine that a Corvette was offered with such nominally meager power. In reality, of course, the old gross horsepower system of 1955 would have tested the 1973 engine at about 225hp, but it was still a depressing situation for the performance hungry.

Owners of this engine today should remember that there is no easier or cheaper V8 than the small block to

Top Left: Base L48 350 with A/C and no power brakes.

rebuild and modify. Without affecting the external appearance of the engine at all, higher compression pistons, larger valves, more aggressive camshafts and gas flowed combustion chambers can improve the performance way beyond anything that was lost back in the early seventies.

The new optional high-performance small block engine for 1973 was the L82, and it was considered a special treat for Corvette owners because no other model apart from the Z28 Camaro was offered with an optional small block engine. Rated at a lower 250hp than the last 1972 LT-1, it at least managed an extra 5lb. ft. of torque at 285 at 4000rpm. This engine would go on to wave the flag for Corvette through the lean years of fuel crises and emission led downsizing and with almost 60,000 units supplied over eight years it is the most popular Corvette optional engine ever.

Left: This 1973 convertible has modified rear lighting for Europe.

SPECIFICATIONS

Wheel-base 98"
Length 15' 6"
Width 5' 10"
Weight 3415 lbs
Transmission 3 speed auto
   or 4 speed manual
Brakes 11.75 disc
Engines
   Base L48 350 V8
   Compression 8.5
   Net Horse Power 195

   Option L82 350 V8
   Compression 9.0
   Net Horse Power 250

   Option LS5 454 V8
   Compression 8.5
   Net Horse Power 270

1974

The LS4 Big Block 454 replaced the 1972 LS5, and gained a nominal 5hp to be rated at 275. At $250 the LS4 was a cheaper option than the $295 L82, and it included a rear sway bar and linkage assembly not otherwise available on the small block cars, unless option ZO7 was chosen. Additionally, big block owners got the new one-piece 454 emblem on either side of the hood, while L82 customers got nothing at all.

The big block adventure was over at the end of 1974. Sales for the final year were just 3,494 but this engine would go on to dominate the motor home market, and developments of it live on in various 4x4s as well. In January 1974, the familiar Muncie 4-speed manual transmission was replaced by the stronger Borg Warner

T-10. This was an updated and strengthened version of the aluminum T-10 last seen in a Corvette in mid-1963. With the muscle car era over, and also because of the ever-rising demand for automatics, General Motors stopped production of high performance manual transmissions. For 1974, the Federal government required that the rear bumper should also withstand a 5mph impact. The same technology was adapted, so that the car could be driven backward squarely into a solid block at 5mph and then be driven away without damage to lights, fuel tank or exhaust. Probably because it was easier to mold, the polyurethane

Left: Tail lamps were recessed to meet Federal crash regulations, nicely matching the style of the recessed speedo and tach.

Above: The simpler fender gill used from 1973 to 1979 allowed more warm air to exit, and saved cost too.

Below: The 1974 rear bumper was unique, made in two halves riveted together, probably the prettiest of all the flexible rear bumpers.

Left: The 1974 nose was the same as 1973, and covered a clever energy absorbing bumper system.

bumper cover was made in two halves held together with aluminum rivets. With no bumperettes or spoilers incorporated, the 1974 tail is surely the most attractive of all the later C4 rears. On the convertible particularly, the long rear deck and smooth tail make an outstanding piece of automotive sculpture, emphasized further by the plain gas filler door, which uniquely to this year had no emblem.

Corvette sales exceeded 30,000 for 1973 and 37,500 in 1974. Unbelievably, the Corvette was still perceived by many as an economy car—scared by the fuel crises, many drivers were downsizing from full size cars to similar engined Corvettes, though many must have realized that at last here was a socially acceptable excuse to drive a Corvette for business!

Above: 1974 was the last year for the 454 big block, now at only 270 hp. It was also the last year for dual exhausts.

Below: A 1974 454 convertible is an extremely rare car, probably only about 500 were built.

Top: A right hand external mirror was not factory fitted , but available over the counter.

Right: The 1974 tail was particularly attractive on the convertible. There was no emblem on the 1974 gas filler lid.

SPECIFICATIONS

Wheel-base 98"
Length 15' 6"
Width 5' 10"
Weight 3530 lbs
Transmission 3 speed auto
  or 4 speed manual
Brakes 11.75 disc
Engines
  Base L48 350 V8
  Compression 8.5
  Net Horse Power 165

  Option L82 350 V8
  Compression 9.0
  Net Horse Power 205

1975

The Federal government were ready with another onslaught on the performance car for 1975. The catalytic converter, it seemed to us at the time, would be fatal to both the Corvette, as the ultimate American V8 performance car, and to the remaining muscle cars. It also seemed that all V8 luxury cars might be doomed as well.

The catalytic converter was chosen by General Motors as the first fix to meet the steep emissions requirements for 1975 model cars. The dual exhaust was diverted into one with a y-pipe, and a catalytic converter was inserted behind it followed by a further y-pipe into two mufflers. The effect on performance was devastating. The power output of the 1975 base L48 engine was 165 horsepower, down 30 from 1974, the lowest since the 1955 155 horsepower straight six and the lowest ever for a Corvette V8.

Confounding the experts and technical press, the Corvette was selling very well although the performance had largely gone. Sales for 1977 were a few hundred short of 50,000. This was the era of the numbing "double nickel" 55mph national speed limit, but the Corvette was quiet, comfortable and economical at this speed and could reach it in under six seconds from a standing start. Appearance, and the selfish appeal of the two-seater, was probably what was selling the Stingray all along and is undoubtedly what attracts most people to them today.

Both the front and rear soft bumper fascias were restyled for 1975, to cover newly designed inner bumper assemblies. The front bumper incorporated new, black-painted over-riders either side of the license plate. These covered stiff rubber buffers that were the first stage of the new bumper system, in which a polyurethane honeycomb absorber was mounted into a support bolted to a main tubular cross bar, which was also used as a vacuum reservoir for the headlight actuators. While the 1973–74 grilles were metal, the 1975 units were plastic and shorter too. At the rear, the fascia unit was now one piece and had small over-riders at the outer ends to match those on the front. The new crash absorber system used an inner bar assembly, which mounted onto oil-filled shock absorbers, designed to take the rear impact.

Catalytic converters needed unleaded gas, so a clear Mylar "Unleaded Gas Only" sticker was affixed to the lower edge of the fuel filler lid. The filler neck itself was now the restricted-size unleaded type too, ending a twelve year tradition of 4-inch filler necks that could not only take a racing size nozzle for faster pit stops and allowed manual cleaning, but—more practically—permitted visual inspection of the fuel available when the gauge became untrustworthy.

SPECIFICATIONS

Wheel-base 98"
Length 15' 6"
Width 5' 10"
Weight 3535 lbs
Transmission 3 speed auto
or 4 speed manual
Brakes 11.75 disc
Engines
  Base L48 350 V8
  Compression 8.5
  Net Horse Power 180

  Option L82 350 V8
  Compression 9.0
  Net Horse Power 210

1976

For 1976 a new air cleaner system drew cold air from a duct arrangement that led to the front of the radiator, replacing the internally ducted hood of 1973–75. The High Energy Ignition (HEI) distributor was an all-new product, and many millions were fitted to General Motors cars during 1975. Although bigger than the contact breaker type unit it replaced, it incorporated the previously separate coil and gave twice the voltage too. Its ability to fire on next-to-no volts was legendary, and it quickly became popular with hot-rodders and racers. It demanded an electronic tachometer, so the engineers took a 90-degree fuel gauge core and added circuitry to increase the deflection of the needle to 310 degrees to match the speedometer. Not surprisingly, failures were common within five years from new, and the needle would often inexplicably stick at 6000rpm. It took almost twenty years for a reliable $95

replacement circuit board to appear on the market, to fix an unnecessary problem. Happily this kind of design is exceptional in the history of the Corvette.

A new steering wheel was fitted for 1976. Much derided as a cheap borrowing from the humble four-cylinder Vega, it was a definite improvement over the thin 1969–1975 wheel. With two cross spokes, it had a smaller but fatter 14-inch diameter rim, and was color co-ordinated to the interior, for the first time since 1963.

1976 saw the much-delayed launch of the eight-slot Aluminum Wheels first proposed in 1973. They were a better-looking alternative to the popular five-slot, after-market wheels fitted to so many cars in the early Seventies, and saved a useful eight pounds unsprung weight per wheel.

SPECIFICATIONS

Wheel-base 98"
Length 15' 6"
Width 5' 10"
Weight 3535 lbs
Transmission 3 speed auto
  or 4 speed manual
Brakes 11.75 disc
Engines
  Base L48 350 V8
  Compression 8.5
  Net Horse Power 180

  Option L82 350 V8
  Compression 9.0
  Net Horse Power 210

1977

The half millionth Corvette was built on March 15, 1977, almost 24 years after the first one rolled off the temporary assembly line in Flint, Michigan. Like that first car, it was Classic White, the third consecutive year that this was the most popular color. It would take just 15 more years to build the millionth car on July 2, 1992.

Bill Mitchell retired in 1977. He bears a massive responsibility for the shape and success of the Corvette. On his retirement the Stingray name was dropped, surely more than a coincidence after his years of promoting the virtues of deep-sea fish. One of his design team, Chuck Jordan, was appointed head of Styling Staff in his place. So for 1977 the Stingray script was now missing from the front fender, and for early production the panel was blank. Then an extended crossed flag, to match the front and rear emblems, was added to either side of the car.

Power steering at last became standard equipment for 1977, still using the "add-on" system first seen on the 1955 Chevrolet, and a new steering wheel was the main change for the driver. The three spokes were brushed stainless steel, with leather to match the interior color stitched over a durable foam rubber rim. For those cars with the regular steering column, a four-spoke wheel very like the 1976 was used. At the same time the steering column was shortened by two inches, allowing a better driving position. 1977s only had a unique multi-purpose turn-signal stalk, which also combined the functions of windshield wash and wipe and headlight dimmer. However, the attempt to combine the functions into one lever was

inept—stalks that were not broken by a slight encounter with a left knee wore out and fell apart due to inadequate design and poor materials.

Cruise control was a new option for 1977, a vacuum mechanical system with a module driven by the speedometer cable. It was one of those markers that showed that the Corvette was becoming more of a personal luxury car and less of a sports car—cruise control had been an option on full size Chevrolets for the previous ten years.

The die-cast, five-clock, center instrument cluster bezel went out in favor of a new black plastic cluster unit, which was designed to accommodate the Corporation's range of in-car entertainment systems. The styling included Allen-head screws round each gauge, giving a nice high tech impression that each gauge could be removed from the front, but sadly the screw heads were fake and just part of the plastic molding. The shift surround console, which was previously die cast metal, was now also plastic, and a pair of more reliable levers replaced the traditional thumb-wheel controls for the heating and optional air conditioning.

GM management must have been tempted to quietly bury the 'Vette when they saw how much the new legislation would affect it. But it was still alive, past the crash test and emissions hurdles and selling more cars than ever. The Press had predicted that by now the power plant would be a V-6 or even a Wankel rotary, and yet we still had the best and most modifiable V8 ever built, powering the best-looking American car of 1977.

Above: The new for 1977 5-gauge cluster was plastic, and the Allen heads were fake.

Above: The shift console was now plastic too, with painted board lower side covers.

Above: The new parking brake console was molded polyurethane. The leather bound aluminum steering wheel was fitted to tilt wheel equiped cars only, leather seats standard for 1977.

Left: This 1977 is fitted with optional 8-slot aluminum wheels and sport mirrors.

SPECIFICATIONS

Wheel-base 98"
Length 15' 6"
Width 5' 10"
Weight 3550 lbs
Transmission 3 speed auto
   or 4 speed manual
Brakes 11.75 disc
Engines
  Base L48 350 V8
  Compression 8.5
  Net Horse Power 185

  Option L82 350 V8
  Compression 9.0
  Net Horse Power 220

1978 Silver Anniversary

The top half of the Corvette had been unchanged for ten years. Now for 1978, designers were looking at the evolution of the Shark, because by adopting the shape of the '63 Split Window, it metamorphosed into and new and better car. The improvement in convenience and luggage space was tremendous. Corvette styling chief Jerry Palmer had looked at the rather tired Corvette and been inspired to do something great with it. The "sugar-scoop" rear window had been a bold statement that had lost its impact—it was sensational in 1968 but was in danger of becoming a trite waste of space by 1977. Originally, the removable rear window had justified the idea of having the glass tight up behind the driver's and passenger's heads, but after 1973, when the window was fixed permanently, the effect had become claustrophobic. By the use of recent glass-forming technology Palmer transformed the car, cheaply enough to convince the management that the Corvette could survive and was worthy of further investment, and well enough to prepare the car for the eighties.

There were two dramatic "Duo Tone" options for 1978. The first was the B2Z Silver Anniversary paint, with a Dark Silver lower half and Silver top half. The accent stripes were all stick-on decals—a total of 18 different stickers. Sport mirrors and aluminum wheels were required options. This color scheme was so popular that it accounted for more than a third of production and, at 15,283 cars painted, it remains the greatest color run of any Corvette year yet.

Right: All 1978s used this 25th Anniversary emblem, regardless of paint color.

Below: The optional L-82 engine had dual cold air snorkels and ribbed aluminum valve covers.

Above: 1978 had a nice new alloy steering wheel with leather trim and new speedo and tachometer.

Wheel-base 98"
Length 15' 6"
Width 5' 10"
Weight 3550 lbs
Transmission 3 speed auto
   or 4 speed manual
Brakes 11.75 disc
Engines
  Base L48 350 V8
  Compression 8.5
  Net Horse Power 185

  Option L82 350 V8
  Compression 9.0
  Net Horse Power 220

1978 Indy Pace Car Replica

The next most popular color was the Limited Edition Pace Car Replica. Originally intended to be limited to just three hundred cars, in celebration of the specially-prepared car that would pace the Indianapolis 500 in May 1978, the final build quantity was officially 6,502. Black over silver, the Pace car used 15 separate stickers. The cars were supplied to the

Above: All Pace Cars Replicas had Silver leather interior and new, actually 1979, seats.

Below: The unique Pace Car wheels had a red stripe and no black paint on their center caps.

dealers with the large "Official Pace Car" sticker for the door, and the small winged-tire Indianapolis Motor Speedway decal for each rear fender rolled up in the luggage area for optional fitting.

Each dealer was assigned a single Pace Car and they were besieged with orders. Enthusiasts who heard early about the Replicas ordered them with their local dealers at list price or a discount. But when some dealers realized what was happening they returned early deposits, while others hiked up the price by thousands. Even options on ordered cars were traded for thousands more. Attorneys litigated, grown men wept, and such was the speculative hype that the story made the front page of the Wall Street Journal on March 27, 1978. Some cars really did change hands for as much as $30,000—the list price was $13,653.21, already much more than the $9,351.89 for the base 1978.

For 1979, the Pace Car spoilers became an option. General Motors claimed that drag was reduced by 15%, to a cd of 0.42, and fuel economy improved.

OFFICIAL PACE CAR
62nd ANNUAL INDIANAPOLIS 500 MILE RACE
MAY 28, 1978

Above: Glass roofs were never a perfect fit, and special care had to be taken when removing them.

Top Right: Between the black top half and the silver lower half there was a red coach line.

The interior makeover that started in 1977 continued for 1978, with a new, one-piece dash panel, containing a new speedometer and tachometer housing for the driver, and a lockable glove-compartment in front of the passenger. Late in 1979 the first of the new 85mph speedometers was fitted in response to Federal pressure to discourage speeding, giving a frightening insight into governmental mindset, and their underestimation of drivers' intelligence.

The new door panels used a corporate GM-design door pull and armrest that was fixed to the steel inner panel of the door with three stout screws. The lower part of the panel was carpeted to match the interior and incorporated small document pockets on each door. These pockets were placed where the window winders had been on non-power window cars. Unfortunately, no one told the door panel designer that power windows were still optional, and cars delivered without power windows had the door winder spindles punched right through the middle of the pockets! On cars with optional cloth seats, this material was also used on the mid part of the door panel. For 1979, the ribbed material was replaced by a hounds-tooth check.

The 1978 seat belt was at last a single-reel design, with the spool mechanism mounted high on the B pillar. Previously, the second reel had been mounted under the seat in a well with no drain, where water from leaking targa roofs accumulated and rusted out the mechanism.

A Citizens Band radio option was added for 1978. This was a fully-integrated, 40-channel AM/FM unit, with a hand-held microphone, and was chosen by 4,483 buyers. This was the peak period of CB enthusiasm, because hereafter sales would drop year by year, until in 1985—the beginning of the cell phone era—just 16 were sold. A power antenna, the first for the C3, was an immediately popular option for 1978.

The base wheel for 1978 was still the Rally wheel, with its large center cap and wide stainless steel outer trim ring, but now only four came with each car because a full-inflated compact spare filled the smaller spare wheel compartment. This was a black painted 15 x 5JJ, with a Goodyear P195/80D15 "temporary use only" tire—a change due to the new larger gas tank.

SPECIFICATIONS

Wheel-base 98"
Length 15' 6"
Width 5' 10"
Weight 3480 lbs
Transmission 3 speed auto
  or 4 speed manual
Brakes 11.75 disc
Engines
  Base L48 350 V8
  Compression 8.5
  Net Horse Power 195

  Option L82 350 V8
  Compression 9.0
  Net Horse Power 225

1979

With the announcement of the Limited Edition Pace Car came an early introduction of the all-new 1979 lightweight seats—for the 1978 Pace Car in Silver leather only. They used a pair of shaped latex foam cushions, wrapped in leather and vinyl, or optionally cloth and vinyl, and clipped into a lightweight molded fiberglass seat, which pivoted half way up the back and folded flat. This facility on the passenger's side allowed quite large loads to be carried.

1978 and 1979 engines are painted blue, and the rule for judging Corvette engines is "Blue means Boring." When you open the hood and see a blue block, you are not looking at automotive excitement. The painfully under-powered sixes of the 1953 and 1954s were painted blue, but the first revolutionary 265 cubic inch, which saved the Corvette in 1955 and later, was a loud orange. Later, all the interesting engines, the fuelies, big blocks and LT1s, were orange too. The dull 75 and 76 motors somehow got painted the same, but for 1977 it was back to blue. It stayed that way through to mid 1982 when, perhaps realizing that the new Cross-fire was actually quite a powerful engine, the blue was banished and—as they say in the fashion world—black became the new orange. The optional L82 was also a repeat of the 1977, but with the new rating of 220hp. At last horsepower was rising again. Otherwise, the L82 recipe was the same—bigger valves, a more aggressive camshaft, 9.0:1 compression ratio forged pistons, selected rods and 4-bolt main bearings. The crank was forged and carried an 8-inch rather than a 6.5-inch harmonic damper.

Starting in 1979, General Electric halogen inner main beam headlamp units were fitted. The Corvette had been under-lit for years, due to ill-considered Federal restrictions on head light candle power and compulsory sealed beams, when the rest of the world was using safer and brighter separate bulb halogen technology. Unfortunately, the restricted space in the headlight capsule still makes it hard to fit the best modern 5 $\frac{3}{4}$ inch separate bulb halogen units.

Above: The L48 350 V8 now gave an honest 195 net horse power. This owner has chrome plated the air cleaner lid, which was normally black until 1981.

Above: A 1979 fitted with L82 V8, now rated at 225 hp.

Left: Both this 1979 and the one above have the optional rear spoiler fitted, but are missing the front full width spoiler which came with the D80 package.

Wheel-base 98"
Length 15' 6"
Width 5' 10"
Weight 3330 lbs
Transmission 3 speed auto
or 4 speed manual
Brakes 11.75 disc
Engines
Base L48 350 V8
Compression 8.5
Net Horse Power 190

Option L82 350 V8
Compression 9.0
Net Horse Power 230

Option LG4 305 V8
Compression 8.5
Net Horse Power 180
(California only)

1980

Of all the C3 series, it is the 1980–82, the ultimate development with its long shovel nose, that is the very essence of a Shark-shaped Corvette.

The 1980 is the last model of the pre-computer age, easy to keep running, tall-geared and economical, and far and way the best looking coupe of the era. It was also the most aerodynamic; the coefficient of drag was 0.443, compared to 0.503 for the spoiler-equipped 1979.

A new, larger, flexible polyurethane molding covered a much lighter, deformable bumper assembly. This incorporated more fiber-glass than previously, and gave the Shark a front-end look in keeping with its nick-name. The front fender was reshaped ahead of the axle center line, and the flexible molding extended all the way to the front wheel.

The hood panel was lower in profile, and made—along with many other panels such as the door skins and the roof panels—of Sheet Molding Compound (SMC). This was a constant thickness, smooth finish, extruded sandwich sheet, delivered uncured, which was laid into the heated matched die presses to form the body panels. Previously, the panels were pressed using labor intensive "preforms."

A lighter rear inner bumper and cushions were hidden by the new tail with the integral "Kamm theory" spoiler. Both bumper units lost the over-riders of the previous five years.

For 1980, the chassis frame was lightened by reducing the thickness of the frame material from 0.110 inches to 0.090 inches, as part of the drastic fuel saving effort for the new decade. Helped by the new front bumper and lighter rear axle, the weight saving on the whole car was about 250lbs. It is probably true to say that the new, lighter frame bent more easily in an accident, particularly at the "S" curves behind the front wheels, but the other improvements surely outweighed this.

The base Corvette engine had been at least 5.4 liter for twenty years, but, for 1980 only, the clean-minded legislators of the Pacific coast had to be appeased with a 5.0 liter engine, the 305ci LG4, which was a foretaste of the 1981. Ignition advance, idle speed and mixture were controlled by an Electronic Control Module (ECM) located in front of the battery. An oxygen sensor was mounted in the left-hand exhaust down pipe—the essential component in a closed loop system, which sensed the state of the burned mixture and told the ECM.

The new 1980 nose and tail reduced drag significantly.

Above: The 1980 interior was unchanged from 1979.

Left: 1980 optional 8-slot alloy wheels had thinner spokes between the slots.

corvette

SPECIFICATIONS

Wheel-base 98"
Length 15' 6"
Width 5' 10"
Weight 3330 lbs
Transmission 3 speed auto
 or 4 speed manual
Brakes 11.75 disc
Engine L81 350 V8
Compression 8.5
Net Horse Power 190

1981

The 1981 engine was the 350 cubic inch version of the California LG4, called the L81. When it came out we were all terrified. With a computer controlling mixture and timing, we felt excluded and redundant. Had the concept of the tune-up lost its meaning? The Assembly Line Diagnostic Link (ALDL) was a multi-plug hidden under the ashtray. But once a Tech-one or Snap-on diagnostic was connected and the car information programmed in, the screen displayed the new world of engine management, the motor could be seen going into closed loop when the oxygen sensor warmed up, the electronic ignition timing was displayed, torque converter lock up demanded, and much more— very quickly we were convinced and converted.

The new Dana aluminum-cased differential, with its own mounting integrated cross-member, was much lighter than the previous iron unit and heavy crossmember that it replaced. Another Corvette tradition—yes it really has been more than twenty years—was first seen on 1981 automatics. This was the new fiber-glass-reinforced, composite rear leaf spring, an idea so successful that it has been used both front and rear since 1984. It weighed only 8lbs., in contrast to the 44lbs. of the nine-leaf steel spring still used on manual transmission and gymkhana-suspension equipped cars. Because there was no inter-leaf friction, the improvement in ride was astonishing, and the spring was also able to move in response to bumps more quickly and effectively too.

1981 saw an important move for the Corvette, from its constricted and run down plant at Natural Bridge Avenue and Union Boulevard in St. Louis, to a fresh start in the warmer climate of Bowling Green, Kentucky, some seventy miles north of Nashville. Cars were produced at both plants simultaneously during June and July of 1981. Twice-daily tours have been a feature at Bowling Green— except during the start-up periods of the C4 and C5 model—and, with the completion of the independently-run Corvette Museum across the street from the new plant, the area has become a magnet for Corvette fans and a major Tennessee tourist attraction.

The ultimate expression of the last C3 Corvette was the beautifully-finished, limited-production Collector Edition Hatchback, but all 1982s are a pleasure to drive. The combination of a truly fuel-injected engine and the new and superb four-speed Turbo Hydra-Matic 700 R4 made this a fast and quiet car in a way that the 1968 never was. With a fine touch for planning, Chevrolet had installed the engine and transmission from the upcoming 1984 C4 Corvette into the last Shark, so that the 1984 would not be too all-new when it was launched. With only an extra five brake horsepower, the 1984 would be a faster car than the 1982, a difference easily explained by its much lower wind resistance.

Above: This 1981 has an after market exhaust system. Millions of dollars are spent annually on modifying Corvettes.

Left: Only the front and rear crossed flag emblems distinguish the 1981 from the 1980 model externally.

SPECIFICATIONS

Wheel-base 98"
Length 15' 6"
Width 5' 10"
Weight 3300 lbs
Transmission 4 speed auto
Brakes 11.75 disc
Engine L83 350 V8
Compression 9.0
Net Horse Power 200

1982

The 1982 Collector Edition Hatchback was finished a unique Silver Beige, or gold if you prefer, fully striped, with fade-out panels on the hood and doors, and special cloisonné Collector Edition emblems. This was the first Corvette to cost more than twenty thousand dollars and it had probably the best of all the interiors from 1968 to 1982. It cost $4247.52 more than the base car, and much of the extra cost went into the interior. Opinions were polarized by the silver-beige and adjacent hues of metallic brown and gray on the seats and door panels, but the Collector Edition Hatchback was still the only Corvette ever sold with leather-covered door panels and a really good quality carpet. It was also the first with an opening hatchback.

Hatchbacks bring with them hinges, remote releases, creaks and leaks. Chevrolet scored no more than a pass

level on any of these, and all give some problems with higher mileages. Luckily a lesson was obviously learned, and the hatchback system fitted to the new 1984 Corvette was superb in every detail, and good enough to last unmodified until 1996.

The aluminum Collector wheel was closely patterned on the 1967 version. With 36 radial fins, it was finished in a similar silver-beige to the car, with the fins clear-coated and polished. Just like the 1967, the plastic starburst cover clipped over, with fins intersecting in the same way to cover the hub and wheel chrome-plated lug nuts.

The 1982 was available only with the new smooth and powerful L83 TBI motor. The new twin injectors worked well on the Chevrolet 350, assisted by yet another cold air induction hood, which connected to the open top of the

twin-filtered, black-crackle-finished air cleaner. Black crackle paint has adorned the engine components of many Corvette dream cars and experimentals, but this is the only production Corvette on which it was used.

The Turbo Hydra-Matic 350 was gone, replaced by the superior TH700 R4, which included an overdrive top gear and a computer-controlled locking torque converter. Third gear was direct, and fourth gave an 0.7:1 overdrive, equivalent to a super tall 36 mph per 1000 rpm in top gear. Comfortable long-distance cruising with a small block has always been better with the motor running at 3,000rpm or less, and now this was equivalent to 108mph it could be truly claimed that Corvette was a long-legged distance machine.

1984-1986

SPECIFICATIONS

Wheel-base 96.2"
Length 14' 9"
Width 6' 2"
Weight 3192 lbs
Transmission 4 speed auto
    or overdrive 4-speed manual
Brakes 11.5 disc
Engine L83 350 V8
Compression 9.0
Net Horse Power 205

1984

During fifteen years of continuous production of the C3 Corvette, and twenty years of producing almost exactly the same chassis, Chevrolet had morphed from manufacturing a cutting-edge fast sports car to a charming classic sports car, while not really changing the product at all. Time and the competition move on, and what was judged fast in 1968 seemed slow by 1982. If the optional thumping big block and high compression big-valved small block engines are ignored, and by the majority of buyers they were, then a comparison of base engined cars from 1968 to 1982 shows only a steady improvement in comfort and driveability. There is nothing wrong with continuity of product, and more than half a million owners of the 1963 to 1982 cars loved the fact that their car was still in production. It helped build the loyalty that has been so important to Corvette, and reassured owners that parts would be available for their cars into the distant future.

But by any assessment the 1982 was old fashioned, and to attract new buyers the next generation Corvette had to be as sensational an advance over its predecessor as the 1963 Sting Ray had been in September 1962. It needed to bridge the performance shortfall that had developed over two decades; too many potential buyers were finding practical if less iconic alternatives to the

CORVETTE

Below: Electric motors powered the headlamp units quickly through 270 degrees of swivel, keeping the lenses clean when hidden.

Corvette—not just the new-for-1982 Z/28 from Chevrolet, but the better built Z cars from Nissan too. The new model needed to be quieter and rattle free, without the wind and water leaks of Sixties frameless window technology. It had to be roomier, with comfortable and fully-adjustable seats, air conditioning and world-class audio, and with enough luggage space for the possessions-rich Eighties consumer. It would need to be environmentally cleaner, as well as much more fuel-efficient to meet the demands of forthcoming legislation—a goal that could only be achieved with drastic attention to aerodynamics and wind resistance. The 1963 Stingray had delivered a staggering improvement in handling over the live axle 1962, while the 1968 was a sensational new body dropped onto the same chassis. Now twenty years on, the new Corvette needed to deliver a similar improvement if it was to regain its reputation as the best mass-produced drivers' car.

Chief Engineer for the project to develop this dream into reality was Dave McLellan, who had been appointed to the Corvette design team in 1975. It is forever to his credit that the C4 Corvette he developed exceeded expectations in every area, and was still a world-class car

when it was replaced after thirteen years with more than 300,000 built. Indeed, in its ZR-1 form it is still arguably the best of all Corvettes to drive, C5 and Z 06 included.

Introduced as a 1984 model in March of 1983, only the L83 5.7 liter V8 engine and Turbo Hydra-Matic 700 R4 automatic transmission were carried over from the previous 1982. Everything else was new and better, and reflected the very best that the vast research and manufacturing facilities of General Motors could offer.

Built on the shortest yet wheelbase of 96.2 inches—the '53 was 102 inches and the '63 was 98 inches—and using specially-developed 255-50 Goodyear "Gatorback" directional tires on 16-inch aluminum wheels, it delivered the nimble handling of a racing kart, along with a cornering force approaching 1.0g. Where the 1963–82 had used existing stamped-steel passenger car suspension and steering components at the front, and a cheap but effective independent suspension at the rear, the C4 had forged aluminum A-arms at the front, and the very latest five-link independent at the rear. Transverse monoleaf fiber-glass springs, like those first used at the rear of the 1981–82, were adopted front and rear for their superb ride, though the initial specification for the '84—particularly with the Z51

Performance Handling Package—was too stiff and it was revised up to 25% softer for 1985. Steering was precise and quick, with a new powered rack and pinion—a Corvette first—or ultra quick, just two turns lock-to-lock, with Z51.

The whole braking system was designed and supplied by Girlock of Melbourne, Australia. Aluminum single-piston front and rear calipers replaced the immense cast iron four-piston units, which had stopped Corvettes since 1965. Fine in normal use, the front discs would overheat and distort if used repeatedly from high speed, a problem that would be resolved in 1988 and was otherwise easily fixed with after-market components.

Above: The 1984 hatch opened higher than previous models , but was later modified because it was too high for some to reach to close.

The striking and sleek body was honed for minimum aerodynamic drag, losing the striking shark curves of the C3, but replacing them with something altogether more subtle. Filled body seams were eliminated, and only the rear upper panels were bonded to the new galvanized uniframe chassis, every other panel being bolted in place. Although the Corvette was often sold as a rust-resistant automobile, the thirty-year dream came true in 1984. A black waistline trim cleverly concealed panel junctions, but the body's best feature was the clam-shell hood, which exposed not only the engine but the entire front suspension too.

Behind a deep windshield, sloped at a streamlined 64 degrees, the driver sat in the first truly adjustable seats ever to be fitted to a Corvette, facing a fully-digital LCD instrument cluster. Switchable between English and metric units, it reported on a full range of functions, including engine oil temperature and average fuel economy. The colored bar graph displays for engine and road speeds were supplemented by digital figures. By agreement with the Federal government since 1979, the speedometer had to finish reading at 85mph to discourage speeding. Cheekily, Corvette's supplementary digital speedo read to 299 mph, and was defended on the grounds that there was no mention in the agreement of a second speedometer! The digital cluster was very popular with owners, but berated by the American press, even when the size of the display digits was doubled and the graphics further improved for 1985. Despite polls showing that owners overwhelmingly preferred digital instruments, the 1997 C5 reverted to gauges because of fears of a bad press.

On the road, the 1984 would reach 142 mph thanks to its 25% better drag coefficient of 0.34. 125 mph was a

practical cruising speed on unrestricted European roads—or for those who dared, on the empty roads of the Southwest. At 75mph the 1984 would easily better 20mpg, and the average fuel economy readout and fuel range prediction also proved to be very accurate in use.

Top: The 1984 205 hp cross five 350 V8 was a carryover from the 1982. The cold air cleaner assembly was fed by ducts in the hood.

Above Left: The fuel filler flap incorporated a lifting recess.

Above Right: All Corvette base wheels are directional from 1984 to 1996. These are left side.

Wheel-base 96.2"
Length 14' 9"
Width 6' 2"
Weight 3192 lbs
Transmission 4 speed auto
or overdrive 4-speed manual
Brakes 11.5 disc
Engine L-98 350 V8
Compression 9.0
Net Horse Power 230

1985

To simplify Corvette model changeovers, General Motors had always preferred to continue the power unit unchanged, and the torquey 205 horsepower Cross Fire introduced for the 1982 was more than adequate for the first year of the C4. It retains a faithful following of fans for its economy and simplicity, but the new Tuned Port Injection engine for 1985 was much more exciting. The Press launch included T-shirts with the logo "Life begins at 150" because this was the fastest base-production Corvette ever, and, with its top speed of 152mph, the fastest American car for fifteen years. Externally, it was identified by Tuned Port Injection text on the front side rubbing strip, and the four exhaust tips that now pointed straight back, instead of down like the 1984.

The secret of the TPI engine's success was its eight-tuned length intake runner, which looped across the engine to give 18 inches of ram effect to the intake air, before mixing with fuel from the eight individual injectors just above each intake valve. While this limited top end power—the motor got a little breathless above 4,500rpm—it gave massive and smooth low end torque, which allowed relaxed cruising at 70mph at under 2000rpm.

150mph in a 1985 Corvette was not the overwhelming tumult of noise and vibration that it would have been in a 1969 427, but a speed easily within the design limits of the car, while 130mph was sustainable until the tank ran dry—and that happens quickly at that speed!

Beneath its clever electronic fuel injection system, the small block engine was still essentially the same unit that had powered the Corvette since 1955. Aluminum cylinder heads had been tried, but were not sufficiently reliable for production in 1959. Now in mid-1986 they were introduced again, using a higher 9.5:1 compression ratio to yield an extra 5 horsepower and save 40lb. engine weight. The heads were easily identified by the four valve cover bolts, which were now in a line down the center of the valve cover rather than at the outside flange, and they were fitted to all the new 1986 convertibles and to late 1986 coupes. Because they conduct heat better than cast iron, the aluminum cylinder heads were less liable to hot spot, and therefore reduced the possibility of pre-ignition, which in turn allowed a higher compression ratio. Almost as if they had the hot rodder in mind, Chevrolet made sure that their aluminum head was a direct bolt-on replacement for the iron version, and would therefore also fit the 1955 car as well, with no modification—no wonder that the Chevrolet V8 is the engine of choice for so many enthusiasts.

In 1984, both manual and automatic transmission cars shared the same aluminum-cased Dana 36 differential, fitted with a $7\frac{7}{8}$ inch crown wheel. While this was strong enough for the automatic, it could not always take the shock of violent use of the clutch, so it was fortunate that

the now legendary and bullet proof 8-inch, ring-gear Dana 44 was fitted to all manual transmission C4 Corvettes from 1985 on. The Dana 36 continued to be used for all automatics until 1996, and it is hard to retrofit the 44.

General Motors had replaced their faithful Muncie transmission with Borg Warner's Super T-10 in the mid Seventies, when production of their own aluminum-cased, 4-speed manual transmission had become uneconomic. Dropped from the Corvette option list at the end of 1981, it now reappeared as a no-cost option on the 1984 model, with the addition of a planetary-geared, two-speed overdrive in place of the tail housing, and calling itself the Doug Nash 4+3 after the company who now built it. This transmission had the advantage of being stronger than the 5-speed used in the Camaro, changed into overdrive mode as soon as the engine reached 150 degrees, and could shift out of overdrive instantly using an automatic-style, kick-down switch out. The overdrive worked on the top three

gears—hence the "4+3"—and could be controlled by a switch on the center console.

The 1985 in particular opened up a whole new market for the Corvette. It was now truly a world-class performance car, absolutely comparable to the best that Ferrari or Porsche could offer, at a fraction of the price and with much lower running costs. Chevrolet started taking quality much more seriously, thanks to the fresh start offered by the 1981 move to the spacious new assembly plant in Bowling Green, Kentucky.

In an inspired move, a permanent telephone help line was established in the plant, manned not by teleworkers or communications students but by supervisors such as Gordon Killebrew with real hands-on assembly line experience, who knew the color of every wire, the number of every circuit and the part number of every relay in the Corvette. This was enormously helpful to dealers' technicians, struggling to come to terms with these high tech, fully-electronic automobiles—and also to the owners and enthusiasts who quickly discovered the phone number. When the help desk got a thank-you call back to confirm a diagnosis, it added to the pool of knowledge about potential problems on higher-mileage cars, and enabled the engineers to incorporate fixes at the build stage.

As a dealer in used Corvettes, the author has always noticed how the C4 buyer would have a series of the cars, while fewer buyers of the 1968 to 1982 cars would buy another. Owners keep saying how they love driving their cars, how they grin whenever they start the engine, how they cannot find enough reasons to take their cars for a drive and, interestingly, how relaxing and stress-free long drives become. This last is surely the result of perfect steering and handling, which renders car control intuitive, a feeling that the drivers of fashionable sports utilities will never experience.

SPECIFICATIONS

Wheel-base 96.2"
Length 14' 9"
Width 6' 2"
Weight 3240 lbs
Transmission 4 speed auto
   or overdrive 4-speed manual
Brakes 11.5 disc
Engine L-98 350 V8
Compression 9.5
Net Horse Power 230

1986

Below: All 1986 convertibles were designated Pace Car Replicas by an emblem on the shifter console, irrespective of external body color.

Anti-lock brake systems have now saved thousands of lives, and the 1986 Corvette was the first GM car to be ABS equipped. Germany had long led research and development of these systems, thanks to their predilection for high speed driving on their unrestricted and often wet or icy autobahns. Using a Bosch design, ABS II, each wheel's speed was electronically monitored. If a wheel was on the verge of lock-up, then the system controlled the braking effort to that wheel, while the driver sensed pulsing through the brake pedal. While it might have been against a skilled driver's instincts, the car could continue to be steered in an emergency if the brake pedal was pressed hard enough to keep the ABS engaged. If history shows a high survival rate for 1986 and later Corvettes, thank Bosch ABS II. 1986 also saw the Corvette fall out of the Most Stolen lists, thanks to the new VATS anti theft system, in which a resistance pellet in the ignition key was checked for one of 15 possible values before the starter, ignition and fuel pump could be energized.

The new 1986 convertible happily continued the tradition of a fully-hidden fabric top that had started with very first Corvette. Beautifully designed and built by the American Sunroof Corporation (ASC) the top featured an inner lining for the first time, a choice of three colors—including a European-style black mohair—and was completely waterproof in use. The steeply-angled windshield of the C4 Corvette was ideal for a convertible, the low turbulence allowing conversation or relaxed stereo listening, while providing excellent wind protection at 70mph. The deck lid was popped open by the same switches that would open the hatch on the coupe, while the fuel filler lid was also specific to the flat rear contour of the soft-top car. To counter fears of convertible shake due to the missing roof structure, a full-size diagonal cross brace was fitted under the car, with additional braces in front and behind the motor, and a brace behind the seats that eliminated the glove boxes. The convertible cost $5,005 more than the coupe, an 18% premium, and despite the late start, made up 21% of 1986 production. Curiously, the convertible has never commanded such a price difference in the used market.

Right: The 1986 convertible top was truly waterproof. Wind deflectors on mirrors were to reduce wind noise.

Left: Only 1986 wheels had a bright center finish

Above: Aluminum cylinder heads, first fitted to 1986 convertibles, were quickly identified by the four in line bolts down the center of each valve cover. Engine and front suspension was superb.

SPECIFICATIONS

Wheel-base 96.2"
Length 14' 9"
Width 6' 2"
Weight 3229 lbs
Transmission 4 speed auto
   or overdrive 4-speed manual
Brakes 11.5 disc
Engine L-98 350 V8
Compression 9.5
Net Horse Power 240

1987

Spotting the new 1987 Corvette was not easy. Only the wheel finish was different to the 1986, with silver-gray center caps and argent silver paint in place of clear lacquer in the central recess. On early production coupes, wind deflectors were fitted to the convertible's mirrors, only to be dropped again on later coupes —either because they were not so effective on the coupe or just to trim a dollar or two from the production cost. External colors were unchanged, but the popularity of the four dual-color options was waning, and they were dropped at the end of the year.

Sales were declining from the peaks of 1984 and 1985, but there was also a marked improvement in quality. The number of cars produced per hour was reduced, so that greater care could be taken with assembly. New 1987s were noticeably quieter and devoid of squeaks and rattles, while the paint finish was also much improved;

indeed from this time on the build-quality of Corvettes improved annually.

Power of the L98 350 increased by 5hp to 240hp, thanks to a new camshaft with roller followers, which also stopped the excessive cam lobe wear that had been an occasional problem since the late seventies. At the same time, the rear main crankshaft seal on the engine was changed to a modern one-piece design, to prevent the characteristic Chevrolet engine oil leak.

On the dash, the overdrive-engaged indicator on manual shift cars was moved to the tachometer sector of the dash, where it was less obvious to the passenger, and was joined by a new upshift arrow. This was switched on by the ECM, when it felt that a higher gear would help save fuel, the environment, and ultimately maybe the motor itself.

The optional Z51 handling package of the previous three years was now subdivided into the Z51

Performance, and Z52 Sport handling packages. Both now used the front frame reinforcements devised to give extra stiffness to the 1986 convertible. Z52 was an immediate hit, being fitted to 40% of 1987 and more than 70% of 1988 production. Best feature of the Z52 Sport package was the quick, 13:1 steering ratio, which worked well with the compliant base specification transverse springs that were controlled by Bilstein shock absorbers and a thicker front sway bar, while the 16-inch wheels were 9.5 instead of 8.5 inches wide. A radiator boost fan and engine oil cooler anticipated high-speed usage. The Z51 package added a heavy-duty radiator and stiff springs, and was limited to manual transmission coupes to prevent it falling into unappreciative hands.

Additional options for 1987 included a passenger seat power seat base, heated mirrors for the convertible, and a driver's side illuminated vanity mirror, so that the increasing proportion of female new-Corvette buyers no longer had to continually adjust the rear view mirror.

1987-1989

SPECIFICATIONS

Wheel-base 96.2"
Length 14' 9"
Width 6' 2"
Weight 3229 lbs
Transmission 4 speed auto or overdrive 4-speed manual
Brakes 12" disc optional 13" front
Engine L-98 350 V8
Compression 9.5
Net Horse Power 240

1988

1988 was the 35th anniversary of Corvette production and a number of significant improvements were made. Most obvious were new 17 x 9½ inch wheels, and 275/40 ZR17 ultra-low-profile tires, which were not optional as such, but were supplied if the car was fitted with either the handling package or the Z01 Special Edition package. These larger wheels permitted new 13-inch front brake rotors on the Z51, with directional internal cooling fins—which were therefore handed left or right. All 1988s were fitted with a new twin-piston caliper from the Australian PBR company. Standard brake disc size increased to 12 inches. Rear calipers now included an ingenious parking brake, spelling the end of the despised separate drum parking brake hidden inside the rear rotor, an unhappy tradition on the Corvette for 23 years. At the time we thought that the troublesome separate shoe parking brake was gone for good, but it reappeared on the 1997 C5, proving that nothing is forever.

Less than 15% of cars used the new six-slot, 16-inch wheel and many of those have since been replaced with original or after-market 17-inch. The 16-inch poor-boy wheels are now very rarely seen, and will soon no doubt become desirable as a result. The 255/50 VR16 tires arguably gave a better ride than the lower aspect ratio 275/40 ZR17s, and they were definitely less prone to aquaplaning, but give us Corvette owners a choice between big and small and we will chose big every time!

To accompany the better wheels and brakes came the first major changes to the all-aluminum suspension. Zero scrub radius was now incorporated into the steering geometry, to improve control and feel. In simple terms this meant that the upper and lower ball joints were positioned outward, with new design A-arms, so that the turning axis of each front wheel was closer to the center line of the tire tread.

American icon the Corvette was, but that alone did not preclude fitting foreign components where they might

ROGER'S CORVETTE CENTER MAITLAND

offer superior performance. So in 1988, the traditional direct drive AC Delco starter motor, which had hardly changed in thirty years, was replaced by a light and compact geared unit from Nippondenso of Japan. Similar weight-saving and efficiency was gained by fitting an air conditioning compressor from the same company. This left the overworked and undersized AC Delco alternator, introduced in 1986, as the single component most likely to fail on any L98 Corvette, as tens of thousand of owners of 1986–1991s have discovered.

The magnificent clam-shell hood was now much easier to open, thanks to a new gas strut which replaced the unassisted telescopic strut of 1986–1987—an item easily retrofitted to the previous C4 models and almost essential on the 1984–1985, which used the weak folding mechanical strut.

In 1988, it was 35 years since Corvette production began with 300 hand-assembled white 1953s. Each of those cars had a red interior—a sensational finish at the time, when tastes were very conservative. To celebrate, 2000 white-option Z01 35th Anniversary Special Editions were built. Perhaps because White was already the second most popular color, and many of those had red interiors, an even more sensational all-white interior was chosen. Impractical for daily use, but ideal for sale to the fastidious Corvette collector, the white theme was used not just on the wheels and door handles, but even on the door armrests and steering wheel. A criticism at the time was that Chevrolet had discovered twelve shades of white and incorporated them all into one car, but the effect was still dramatic, and the three-circled side emblem that combined the 1953 and 1988 logos was one of the best ever. The same logo in miniature adorned the gearshift console, next to a sequential Special Edition build number.

SPECIFICATIONS

Wheel-base 96.2"
Length 14' 9"
Width 6' 2"
Weight 3225 lbs
Transmission 4 speed auto
or 6-speed manual
Brakes 12" disc
optional 13" front
Engine L-98 350 V8
Compression 9.5
Net Horse Power 240

1989

Externally, the 1989 Corvette was identical to the majority of 17-inch wheel equipped 1988s, but once again there were many changes and improvements. By far the best was the new six-speed manual transmission, again the best available and bought in like the fuel injection and ABS systems from Germany—this time from Zahnradfabrik Friedrichshafen AG, better known as ZF. This was a superb transmission, capable of handling 450lbs.ft. of torque but with a sweet shift. It was fully synchronized, even in reverse, making parking maneuvers easy and giving a real advantage to the autocross and gymkhana competitors who could now engage reverse smoothly, even while still travelling forward.

The Federal authorities still managed to influence even the design of a gearbox, and to achieve acceptable fuel consumption a "skip shift" device was incorporated into the new six-speed. Called CAGS, for computer aided gear selection, it forced the shift lever to select 4th rather than 2nd gear after a pulling away in first. If the ECM sensed less than 35 degrees of throttle angle, engine temperature at more than 120°F and a road speed of 12–19mph, then the ECM energized the plunger that blocked the engagement of 2nd gear. Fortunately, this infuriating device was also easily disabled by disconnecting a plug on the side of the transmission case.

Rumored as a possibility since 1987, a low-tire pressure warning system—inevitably known by the acronym LTPWS—was on the option list for 1989, and was fitted to almost one quarter of cars built. Each wheel transmitter was powered by a piezo ceramic device, which generated power from the rotation of the wheel. The receiver was mounted under the dash. Not only did it make sure that owners kept their tires up to a safe pressure for daily driving, it also warned of low tire pressure at very high speeds—where centrifugal force can keep a punctured tire in shape with little or no internal air pressure, only for the driver to discover a major problem when the tire overheats or he slows for a bend. Retained into the well of the rim by a large hose clip with an opposed counterbalance weight, its only real problem was damage caused by tire fitters who failed to read the warning sticker on the outside edge of the wheel rim.

The Z52 Sport Handling package, so popular in 1988, was dropped in favor of FX3 Selective Ride and Handling. This was made possible by Delco/Bilstein shocks, which incorporated adjustable valves controlled by a stepper motor on top of each shock absorber. A three-way knob behind the gearshift offered three positions: Tour, Sport and Perf(ormance). It was limited to cars with Z51 and six-speed transmission, but used the softer Z52 transverse road springs. It was very impressive and acceptably reliable, the weak point being the motor units, which were prone to sticking after attack by road spray.

In its fourth year of production, the convertible was at last offered with a detachable hardtop. Costing almost $2000, it was beautifully made. It could not be fitted to another non-hardtop convertible without transferring the specific fittings at the windshield and brackets from the rear quarter. Because these have long since been discontinued, a hard top without the fitting kit is effectively useless. At the same time soft-top buyers were offered an ingenious rear luggage rack which incorporated a mini-spoiler.

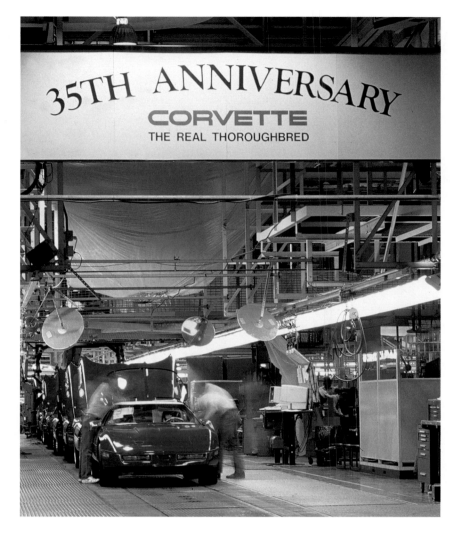

SPECIFICATIONS

1991 Callaway
Wheel-base 96.2"
Length 14' 10"
Width 6' 2"
Weight 3440 lbs
Transmission 6-speed manual
Brakes 12" disc
  optional 13" front
Engine twin turbo 350 V8
Net Horse Power 403
Peak Torque 575 lb-ft

1987–91 Callaway

Determined to make the most of their outstanding new chassis, Chevrolet had been working on various ultra-high performance versions of the Corvette since soon after its 1983 introduction. Forced induction with turbo or superchargers was an obvious option, while development of a high revving version of the small block, with multiple cams and more than 16 valves, was another. It was decided to take both paths—Lotus Engineering of Norfolk, England were commissioned to design an all-aluminum 375hp 4-cam 32-valve engine for a 1989 introduction, of which more later, while Callaway Engineering, of Old Lyme, Connecticut, would produce a series of twin-turbocharged 345hp cars as a Regular Production Option (RPO) B2K. Callaways were built as regular cars at Bowling Green, then transported to Connecticut for modification before delivery to the Chevrolet dealer. They could be coupe or convertible, with manual transmission only, and delivered an amazing 465lb.ft. of torque.

184 were delivered in 1987, these cars being notable for their twin NACA ducts on the hood for their intercoolers. Power was boosted for the 124 1988 cars—382 hp at 4250rpm and 545lb.ft. of torque at only 2750rpm. The intercooler ducting was now built into the hood, British Dymag 17-inch wheels were included, and the price of the option was up to $25,895 from $19,995 in 1987. The following year only 69 were sold, as the market anticipated the expected ZR1, which was not finally launched until 1990.

The Callaway was a car of entirely different character to the ZR1, but just as desirable. It continued as a production option alongside the ZR1 for 1990 and 1991, but thereafter Callaway dealt direct with their customers, and went on to more great thing with Corvettes, which are outside the scope of this book.

Above and Left: This 1989 Callaway was returned to Old Lyme in 1993 to have the Callaway Aerobody fitted, and then later modified by them to incorporate special double ducted intercoolers. It has been timed at 215mph on a closed track.

SPECIFICATIONS

Wheel-base 96.2"
Length 14' 9"
Width 6' 2"
Weight 3255 lbs
Transmission 4 speed auto
    or 6-speed manual
Brakes 12" disc
    optional 13" front
Engine L-98 350 V8
Compression 9.5
Net Horse Power 245

1990

Apart from attractive and lighter new 17-inch wheels, the 1990 Corvette had the same external appearance as the 1989—but a glance into the interior or under the hood showed that much was revised. The new interior followed from the legal necessity to fit the Corvette with a driver's air bag—in GM-speak an SIR or Supplemental Inflationary Restraint. This was a GM invention of many years previous. In 1994, a passenger-side air bag would be mandatory too, so the dash, instrument cluster, steering wheel and door panels were redesigned to accommodate the changes. A lockable glovebox was supplied in the space reserved for the 1994 passenger's airbag.

Corvette was the first two-seater, and the first American car to be available with seat belts way back in 1956. Most Corvette owners always wear their seat belts—just as no racing driver would go out onto the track unbelted, they are part of the culture of driving enjoyment. Unfortunately there is an underclass of road users—none of whom is likely to read this—who hate driving, drive badly while deriving no pleasure from their cars, and are too lazy to wear their seat belt but quick to get litigious when injured through their own folly. All cars now had to be designed to protect the foolish minority, and the Corvette was to be no exception.

The SIR was a complex system and, together with another Federal requirement, On Board Diagnostics (OBD), demanded a whole new level of electronics. This was introduced with the incorporation of a second computer, known as the central control module (CCM), which was buried centrally in the dash, ahead of the stereo console. A new and larger ECM was moved to a new under-hood position above the battery. The CCM controlled all the functions of the new dash, including odometer, trip, speed and fuel-use management, English/metric displays, chimes, anti-theft systems, courtesy lighting, and many other functions.

Now it was possible to check for all body computer CCM fault codes, both current and historic, by pressing the ENG/MET and TRIP/ODO buttons on the console. Information was

displayed via the trip and speedometer digital displays, and a full range of CCM data could be viewed as well. CCM malfunctions were alerted by an "SYS", for system error, flashing on the display, while ECM problems were still signaled through a "check engine" message on the information console. Most ABS brake problem codes could also be displayed on the same screen, after grounding pin H of the ALDL connector.

The new dash reverted to old-technology swing needle gauges for minor engine functions, so that only the speedometer, trip, and fuel range and average functions were available in a choice of metric or English units. It was an essential change to allow the instruments to be seen through the large steering wheel center, which now contained the airbag module. Unusually located on the door since 1984, the wiper switch was now moved to the turn signal switch. The steering column lost the telescopic adjustment, but the dash gained a useful "oil life" monitor display thanks to the power of the new CCM, which

assessed oil temperature and engine revolution history to calculate when an oil change was required.

The Bose radio system was now offered with a CD player, doubled in power output to 200 watts, and the front speaker amplifier enclosures were moved from within the doors to the floor. Too many had been ruined by rain flowing through the door, and this was a welcome improvement. Best of all, it now had speed-related automatic volume control, even adjustable for roof on or off. Unnoticed at first, it only becomes apparent how good it is when you find yourself constantly adjusting the volume in the next car you drive!

This was definitely the most electronic 'Vette yet. Technicians sometimes struggled, and the Bowling Green help desk rallied with their support. Once again it seemed that electronic complications were overwhelming the Corvette, but a decade later a new generation of electronically-savvy home mechanics is happily coping with trouble codes and digital voltmeters that would have stumped their parents.

Under the hood, the sometimes-frail mass air flow sensor and cold start injector was replaced with a speed density system, in which more ECM power calculated the fuel air ratio instead. Engine output was up another 5 horsepower, thanks to this and camshaft changes. The radiator was now sloped back, which improved cooling and had an additional benefit about which Corvette engineers expressed surprise—although they may have known exactly what they were doing. It reduced the Corvette's radar image to the best of any American car, almost making it into a stealth vehicle on the highway, because the only significant metal in the front of the car was reflecting the radar transmission up into the sky instead of back into the into radar gun! Incorporated with the new cooling system was an additional high-level coolant header tank, solving the difficulties sometimes experienced when filling the previous system directly into the radiator.

SPECIFICATIONS

Wheel-base 96.2"
Length 14' 10"
Width 6' 2"
Weight 3255 lbs
Transmission 4 speed auto
  or 6-speed manual
Brakes 12" disc
  or optional 13" front
Engine L-98 350 V8
Compression 10.0
Net Horse Power 245

1991

In its thirteen-year life span the C4 Corvette received only one exterior makeover and this happened in 1991. In this Chevrolet were assisted by body styling specialists Hawtal Whiting, who were based in Coventry, England, and had worked on the packaging and mock-ups of the Lotus-designed ZR-1 and the styling of the LT5 engine. Under the direction of GM Design, they continued the theme set in the unique convex 1990 ZR1 tail, by adapting this in a narrower version for the L98 powered car, and matching it to a more streamlined nose with a wraparound effect to the fog-light park light units and the side marker turn lamp units. The body side moldings were made wider and finished in the body color, while the side vents behind the front wheels were given a horizontal treatment. The coupe's high-level brake light was moved into the rear fascia, where it had always been on the convertible. These changes added 2 inches to the overall length of the car, all the extra being in the new tail molding, making the car virtually the same length as the ZR-1. The front and filler cap emblems were also slightly revised, while the rear Corvette name was now molded into the bumper.

Starting with the 1963 knock-off wheel, all directional Corvette wheels have pointed "forward" in relation to their direction of travel. The new-for-1991 wheel reversed this tradition, and also inexplicably used a different diameter snap-in lug on its center cap—although the exterior diameter remained the same—reducing interchange ability. The wheel itself looked superb, and was now made in Japan. All previous Corvette wheels—even back to 1953—were made by GM's own Kelsey Hayes.

An additional new convenience for the driver waiting in the car was delayed accessory power, which would leave the radio playing and the windows operable for up to fifteen minutes after the key was turned, and was cancelled by opening the door. General Motors was also suffering an increasing number of problems from badly-installed cellular phones, so a specific 12-volt accessory wire was supplied at the center console for just this purpose.

Dropped from the option list after seven years was the hard-riding Z51 suspension, to be replaced by Z07. This combined the stiff springs of the previous option, with the sophistication of the switchable FX3 selective ride and handling.

Left: A new dash was required beecause of the airbag steering wheel.

Below: 1991 was the last year for the 245 hp L98 V8 350.

Left: A new nose and tail for 1991 increased overall length by 1".

1992

Chevrolet have always been skilled at maximizing the impact of their annual updates and improvements. If you had saved for years to buy the 'Vette of your dreams and finally bought the manual transmission in 1985, you might well have thought of trading it in to get the ABS brakes of 1986, the desirable aluminum cylinder heads of 1987, the 17-inch wheels and better brakes of 1988, the must-have six-speed transmission of 1989, the all-new interior and CD player of 1990. If you relented and bought the 1991 because of its great new exterior styling, then you would have been mad at yourself in 1992 because that year brought with it perhaps the most significant improvement in the C4's thirteen year history—the 300 horsepower LT-1. This was a full 50 horsepower improvement in output, the biggest increase in years and the most powerful base engine ever, if the high gross horsepower figures of the sixties are corrected to the comparable net figure.

Not as pretty as the Tuned Port Injection L98 which it replaced, the LT1 lacked the swooping intake tubes, but it packed a solid 300 horsepower, thanks mainly to the highest compression ratio used in a small block since 1970. At 10.5:1, it was a dream come true for those who lived through the dull years of the mid-Seventies, when the 9.0:1 L82 was as exciting as things got. The 11.0:1 LT1 of 1970 could only run thanks to the easy availability of high-octane fuel, rich in Tetra-ethyl lead, which prevented pre-ignition. This fuel was quickly phased out in the early seventies, and all gasoline was lead-free after 1978. Now the new LT1 of 1992 would handle very low-octane fuel, thanks partly to the better conduction of the aluminum head, but mainly due to the wonders of knock-sensing electronic timing and reverse flow cooling.

The latter was a spin off from the LT5 engine development. Coolant traditionally, and naturally via

convection, flows up through the hot engine and down through the radiator. The engineers at Lotus realized that the cylinder heads could be more efficiently cooled if they were the first part of the engine to receive the coolant from the radiator, rather than the last—and that this was easily achieved with a more powerful water pump, which was now positively-driven by an extension of the camshaft, instead of by the accessory belt as previously.

The same drive that spun the water pump was also used to drive the front mounted ignition distributor on the LT1. All previous small block distributors had been driven from the rear of the camshaft, and it made sense to tuck this item behind the water pump at the front of the engine, if only to enable the LT1 to be fitted in to the 1993–2002 Chevrolet Camaro.

Unfortunately, water pump failure or flooded roads meant that the new high tech Opti-Spark distributor got soaked, and unless it was quickly dried out replacement was the only cure. It also suffered from internal condensation, due to inadequate venting. Improved breathing arrangements as production proceeded only partly solved the problem, but the smoothness and extra power from the more accurately-timed spark made it all worthwhile.

Under the hood, a new box marked ASR signaled the advent of traction control for the Corvette. Acceleration Slip Regulation was GM's more technically correct name for their version of this technology, which was once again developed by Bosch. Using the existing rear wheel ABS sensors, the system could detect the onset of wheel spin and would simultaneously brake the slipping wheel, retard the ignition spark and relax the throttle. The device under the hood was the throttle cable relaxer motor, which would also push back the throttle pedal, telling the driver that the system was operational. While the ASR could be switched off for the driver who wanted full wheel spin—such as for the drag strip or for track use—it made it possible to drive more positively and faster when roads were wet, enabling more power to be used, for instance, when pulling out onto a wet main road. Aggressive drivers are still surprised how quickly the system will use up rear brake pads, but ASR was a real advance for the Corvette, allowing it to be driven faster while making it still safer.

At the rear, bold new rectangular exhaust outlets recalled the similar trims on the 1970–1973 Corvettes. There were more changes further forward in the system too. Twin oxygen sensors and twin low-restriction catalytic

converters lead the exhaust into an ingenious resonator box, which kept each bank's exhaust gases separate before they exited through the new-design mufflers. So for the first time since 1974, the Corvette had a true dual exhaust system again.

Goodyear had been the exclusive vendor of tires for the model since 1978, following the Firestone 500 debacle and recall. The directional Goodyear Eagle Gatorback had been used since 1984, first in 16-inch and then 17-inch versions. Now these were replaced, by the same manufacturer's improved directional and asymmetric Eagle GS-C in the same 275/40 ZR17 size. As with the 1984 Gatorback, the Corvette had a year of exclusive use of the tire before it was offered to other manufacturers. The asymmetric design recognized that the outer tread performed a different function to the inner during cornering, but this also meant that left or right tires had to be ordered when replacement was due. Sounds tricky? Read on to see what happened in 1993!

Inside the car there were minor changes to the instruments. The digital speed readout moved up above the fuel gauge, and a new "gauges" button replaced the previous "range." Fuel range was still available by cycling though the "fuel" button readouts, but the new "gauges" button now restored to the screen the digital engine readouts that had been unhappily lost with the changeover to the new dash two years previously.

Less than forty years previously, the first few white 1953 Corvettes, with their red interiors, had been hand-assembled in Flint, Michigan. Now, on July 2, 1992, the millionth Corvette—appropriately also a white convertible—left the final assembly area at Bowling Green, Kentucky. Better still, it was donated to the new National Corvette Museum, on which construction had started just across the road from the assembly plant only a month previously.

Top: By 1992 convertibles were accounting for one third of sales.

Left: This convertible had GM made tail lamps and added reflectors to pass German inspection.

Bottom Left: The New LT1 engine gave a full 300 bhp and was redlined at 5700 rpm.

Bottom Center: This Airbag steering wheel and new dash date from 1990.

Bottom Right: A clever optional luggage rack features an aerofoil rear bar.

Wheel-base 96.2"
Length 14' 10"
Width 6' 2"
Weight 3335 lbs
Transmission 4 speed auto
  or 6-speed manual
Brakes 12" disc
  or optional 13" front
Engine LT1 350 V8
Compression 10.5
Net Horse Power 300

1993

The buyer of a 1992 Corvette could look at the specifications of the 1993, and see to his relief that there was, for the first time in years, not too much that would make him wish that he had waited for the new model. Externally it was noticeable that the rear wheels were larger than the front, much like the ZR1, but not so exaggerated. Indeed Press releases suggested that it was to "balance tractive efforts," but the 824 Z07 cars came with the rear wheel size all round. More likely the small front tires, 255/45 ZR17 mounted on 17 x 8.5 wheels, were a way to reduce frontal area and rolling resistance in the noble quest for better fuel consumption and a reduction in the Corporation's average fuel economy. Rear tires were 285/40 ZR17, a half-inch or 10mm wider than 1992. The 1993 owner, faced with replacing his asymmetric Goodyear Eagle GS-Cs, soon found out that his car needed four different and non-interchangeable tires, causing endless scope for confusion at the tire shop, and headaches for those seeking to keep a good stock of Corvette rubber.

It was now the fortieth birthday of the Corvette, and almost a third of production was ordered in the optional 1993 40th Anniversary livery, which consisted of Ruby Red metallic paint, matching Ruby leather sport seats and interior, special emblems, and red center caps in the wheels. All seats, except the base cloth, had the 40th logo embroidered into the head rest. Like the 35th Anniversary before, the 40th also had special emblems at the rear of the hood in front of the doors. Under the hood, the LT1 motor lost a little more of its glitter when new sound-attenuating polyester valve covers replaced traditional aluminum. Minor cam and exhaust manifold cover changes also served to reduce noise.

Passive Keyless Entry (PKE) was the electronic novelty for 1993. American designed, it used two concealed antennas to sense proximity of the key fob, which could be in the driver's pocket, to unlock the car as it was approached, or lock it and honk the horn as the driver walked away. This was an ingenious and popular system, though noisy from the constant horn honking when washing the car, until the owner learned how to turn off the system by holding the door button down beside the car until the locks cycled.

Above: The 350 V8 delivered 300 net hp.

Above: 1993 interior.

Below: The 1992–1996 LT1.

Wheel-base 96.2"
Length 14' 10"
Width 6' 2"
Weight 3335 lbs
Transmission 4 speed auto or 6-speed manual
Brakes 12" disc or optional 13" front
Engine LT1 350 V8
Compression 10.5
Net Horse Power 300

1994

While the exterior of the 1994 coupe was the same as the 1993, the convertible gained a heated glass rear window, replacing the flexible Ultrashield used since 1990. By contrast there were considerable improvements to the interior. Firstly the seats—in particular the sport seats, which were often criticized by all but the slimmest of owners for being too tight—were changed to accommodate a broader profile of driver. The extra function switches for the sport seats were moved from the edge cushions to the center console.

Federal law required a passenger-side airbag for 1994, and this was incorporated into the previous glovebox. The door panels were redesigned to incorporate a useful lidded compartment in each armrest instead. The air conditioning system was changed to run on environmentally-friendly R134-A, instead of the more efficient R12 Freon, itself a GM invention.

The mass airflow sensor, eliminated for 1990, made a comeback for 1994 in an improved version. It was linked to a more sophisticated sequential fuel injection system, which triggered the injectors in sequence with the firing order, improving smoothness and driveability. Engine management was now controlled by a Powertrain Control Module (PCM), which replaced the ECM and integrated the functions of the new electronic shift 4L60-E transmission. As a safety precaution, and in line with other manufacturers, it was now necessary to press the brake pedal before the transmission could be released from park.

Right: Front parking lamps with special lenses, amber side repeaters fitted behind the front wheels, and British made folding back mirrors for pedestrian safety. The radio tunes to even as well as odd numbered frequencies and seat belts were European sourced and came only in black.

Above: This rare 1994 was factory built with the full export kit. A special rear fascia had shallower mounting for the back lights, integrated rear reflectors below the bump strip, an extra wide rear license plate aperture and flares over all four wheels so that the tires didn't protrude from the body.

SPECIFICATIONS

Wheel-base 96.2"
Length 14' 10"
Width 6' 2"
Weight 3335 lbs
Transmission 4 speed auto
    or 6-speed manual
Brakes 13" front
    12" rear
Engine LT1 350 V8
Compression 10.5
Net Horse Power 300

1995

New gill panels behind the front wheels were the only significant exterior change on the 1995. Reminiscent of similar trims on the 1962, they were a reminder that, just as then, the model was on the runout to something altogether new and better, but still secret. The exception was the dramatic Indianapolis Pace Car Replica. Only 527 were built, making this one of the rarest Corvettes ever. All were automatic transmission convertibles, dark purple over white, with flowing flag graphics and a white convertible top. Interiors were black leather with a special logo embroidered into the headrest. Wheels were the five-spoke front 17-inch x 9.5-inch A-Molds, first used on the 1994 ZR1. To buy one of these cars you needed to be a close friend, or very good customer, of one of the 415 top Corvette retail dealers of 1994 who were eligible be offered the saleable Pace Car Replicas. The remaining 87 cars were retained for activities in connection with the May 1995 race.

Reverse gear on manual transmission cars could now be engaged without lifting a lockout device, a feature of all four-speeds since 1959, although the rare three-speed survived without this feature until its demise in 1969.

Instead, a stronger spring was added to resist inadvertent engagement of reverse gear.

Goodyear's Eagle GS-C Extended Mobility Tires (EMT), were first optioned in 1994. These reinforced sidewall tires offered up to 200 miles driving after a puncture, at a maximum speed of 55 mph. Cleverly, they fitted the stock rim. Now a new 1995 option, spare tire delete, offered a $100 credit and a substantial weight saving to buyers prepared to put their trust in the new technology. The EMT tires were noisier than the normal GS-Cs but were destined to become the standard tire, with no spare back up, on the new C5 model from 1997. ZR1s and Z07 equipped cars had 13-inch front brake rotors as standard, handed because of their directional internal finning, while all others used a 12-inch rotor. All Corvettes from 1995 on now used the 13-inch heavy-duty units.

SPECIFICATIONS

Wheel-base 96.2"
Length 14' 10"
Width 6' 2"
Weight 3335 lbs
Transmission 4 speed auto
  or 6-speed manual
Brakes 13" front
  12" rear
Engine LT1 350 V8
Compression 10.4
Net Horse Power 300

Option LT4 V8
Compression 10.8
Net Horse Power 330

1996 Collector edition

Like its Silver Anniversary predecessor of 1978, the Sebring Silver 1996 Collector Edition was the most popular color for the year, making this the only year of C4 production in which red was not the favorite color, Anniversary Ruby Red displacing Torch Red in 1993. Like the Grand Sport, the Collector used the five-spoke A-Mold wheels, this time in silver and only in the smaller widths. The car was available in manual LT4 or auto LT1 versions, and with black, gray or red interior and special Collector Edition emblems.

To make the most of this engine, the memorable Grand Sport was built in a limited edition of just 1000.

The ZR1 was last year's model and yesterday's news in 1996, so there was no restriction on the advocates of the traditional pushrod small block engine from celebrating the home-grown American product with a special 10.8:1 compression ratio 330 horsepower LT4.

Only available with the manual transmission, and the required engine if the six-speed was specified, this motor was only 45 horsepower short of the 1990 to 1992 specification ZR1.

Recalling the briefly glorious career of Zora Arkus-Duntov's five 1963 Grand Sport racers, these Admiral Blue cars had a white race stripe, red hash marks on the left front fender, and a black, or black and red, interior. There were 190 convertibles and 810 coupes built, all with a unique series serial number. Wheels were a black painted version of the ZR1's 17-inch A-mold, 8.5-inch front and 9.5-inch rear on the convertible, and 9.5-inch front and 11.5-inch rear on the coupe. Because these ZR1 wheels protruded beyond the arches on the coupe, they were fitted with bolted-on rear fender flares, which had been developed for European export versions of the early 1990s cars. With the red seats, red fender hashes and special badges, this one of the most unlikely yet attractive Corvettes ever built.

Two suspension options made the list for 1996, the ultra sporting Z51 was revived after a five year break and a new and expensive F45 Selective Real Time Damping (RTD), replaced FX3 Selective Ride. Anticipating the system that would be a popular option on the forthcoming C5, this used individual position sensors ahead of each hub, mounted between the body and upper A-Arm at the front, and the body and lower trailing arm

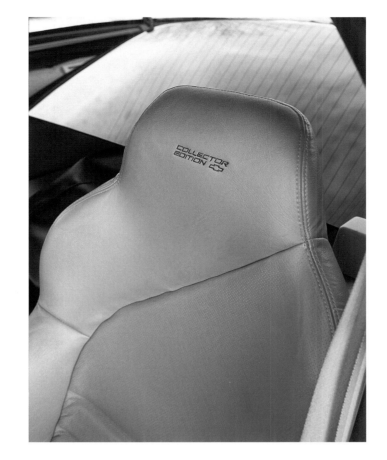

at the rear. Input from these sensors was processed by the RTD module, influenced by the driver's 3-position switch and the vehicle speed, to vary the valving of each individual shock many times a second. To give an idea of the complexity of the system, it takes 90 pages to cover it in the 1996 shop manual although the entire engine rebuild section is only 149 pages, but in service it is remarkably reliable.

Right: The Grand Sport used ZR1 type 5-spoke wheels finished in black. On the Coupe they were ZR1 width with add-on flares.

Below: The Silver Anniversary was so popular that it displaced red as the favourite color for this C4 year only.

Right: While the base LT1 engine remained at 300 hp, manual cars were fitted with an LT4 rated at 330 hp.

Above: Improved and larger seats, which 'accommodated a wider range of occupant sizes', had been introduced in 1994.

SPECIFICATIONS

1990-1995 ZR1

1990 ZR1
Wheel-base 96.2"
Length 14' 10"
Width 6' 2"
Weight 3479 lbs
Transmission 6-speed manual
Brakes 13" front
    12" rear
Engine LT5 350 V8
Compression 11.0
Net Horse Power 375
Max Torque 370 lb-ft

1995 ZR1
Wheel-base 96.2"
Length 14' 10"
Width 6' 2"
Weight 3512 lbs
Transmission 6-speed manual
Brakes 13" front
    12" rear
Engine LT5 350 V8
Compression 11.0
Net Horse Power 405
Max Torque 385 lb-ft

ZR1

More than 75% of the ZR1 was just stock Corvette parts, it was produced on the same assembly line at Bowling Green as the standard car, it was only about 30mph faster than the regular car, and from 1992 on the LT1 engine was rapidly approaching the power of the LT5. So how does the ZR1 deserve a chapter all to itself?

The answer becomes obvious the moment you get behind the wheel and drive one. In any era there have been cars which stand out from the mass, exceptional machines that are as satisfying to drive today as when they were built years ago. The ZR1 is one of those, developed by enthusiastic engineers, with an almost unlimited budget, in an extraordinary transatlantic partnership that melded the best of English and American skills.

In 1985 it was obvious to the design team that in the Corvette, Chevrolet had chassis-and-suspension combination that could easily handle more power than even extreme development of the iron block 350 small block was likely to yield. Tests with twin turbochargers proved what an outstanding car a 185mph Corvette could be, but a turbocharged car is an uncompromising beast, and McLellan and his team wanted something that would deliver the same ultimate performance, combined with quiet tractability, smoothness, fuel economy and exemplary emissions. Working with specialist engine technologists at Lotus Engineering in Norfolk, England—a company which General Motors subsequently bought—the 4-cam 32-valve

all-aluminum V8 was a frantic four years in development. The resulting 375hp LT5 motor fulfilled all that was expected of it. Initially a batch of 20 1989 ZR1s were built, and fifteen of these were used for the world launch of the model at the Geneva Motor Show on March 7th 1989, and for an extended test drive for a group of America's leading auto magazine publishers—who not surprisingly loved the new car as they tested it through France.

Left: The 1990 ZR1 was the same as the base L98 from the front.

The first saleable ZR1s were all 1990 models, with the new 1990 dash and wheels, but such was the publicity from the launch that published pictures of the car often show the 1989—the ZR1 that was never sold. As many as 84 may have been built for publicity, and engineering development and evaluation, as were the first 20 or so of 1990 cars.

The beauty of the LT5 engine was the extraordinary range of response it offered. It could drive you gently through the suburbs all week, with fuel economy better than the L98, and then spend a weekend at the track revving to 7000rpm. The car immediately became a target for tuners, who could easily raise the power output to 600bhp, which then demanded bigger brakes, noisier free-flowing exhausts

and stiffer coil over-suspension, in place of the fiberglass transverse springs. These tuned cars often had genuine 200mph performance, but threw away the greatest virtue of the ZR1, which was its extraordinary dual personality—from quiet cruiser to roaring beast in a moment. With a stock ZR1 you could leave the suspension switched to "tour" and the valet key off and you got a car that was hard to distinguish from the base L98, quiet, comfortable and refined, but twist those two clockwise and the beast was revealed. The sound and feel of the all-aluminum LT5 was entirely different to the cast iron small block at higher revs, as different as a Harley and Ducati V-Twins.

The engines were assembled by Mercury Marine in Stillwater, Oklahoma, who had unrivalled experience of manufacturing lightweight high-revving and powerful inboard and outboard motors for boats. The cylinder block was cast in Texas, the plenum and oil pan in Missouri, while the cylinder head, connecting rods, and crankshaft came from the UK. The pistons, rings and cylinder liners were made by Mahle of Germany.

Below Left Top: The Lotus designed 32 valve 4 cam engine fitted into same space as the single cam pushrod L98. This is a 1989 press car.

Below Left Bottom: Each LT5 motor was tested on the dyno at Mercruiser's Stillwater assembly plant.

Below: Chief engineer for Corvette from 1975-1992, Dave McLellan has arguably had more influence on Corvette history than his predecessor Duntov. He was the driving force behind the improved 1980-82, the architect of the C4, the father of the ZR1 and the originator of the C5. Since he took over, every year of Corvette has been better than the last. He deserves our thanks more than anyone else in the fifty years of Corvette.

Apart from the entirely new and different all-alloy 375 horsepower motor, the ZR1 was essentially a stock 1990 Corvette as far back as the doors and through the cabin. Indeed, from the front, only the purplish reflective hue of the windshield gave a clue to identify the car. This Koolof screen, made by LOF, had an anti-solar reflective finish, which would also prevent the use of a radar detector. A clear panel was therefore incorporated in the lower part of the screen, which Chevrolet said was for a garage door transmitter, but us ZR1 owners of course know better!

Such was the power of the ZR1, that bigger rear tires were needed to put the power to the ground. Goodyear 315/35 ZR17 tires were mounted on an 11-inch version of the 1990 wheel, which in turn required wider rear body work to cover them. So the ZR1 doors were made with a taper out to the rear, the rocker panel and rear fenders were unique, and an entirely new convex rear bumper fascia completed the package. With export markets in mind, this rear molding was made with a large license plate recess and new-shaped rear lamps which, for

the first time since 1973, used separate lenses to simplify bulb replacement.

3,049 ZR1s were sold in 1990, and only 2,044 in 1991. It didn't help sales that the economy was in recession, but worse for the buyer who wanted his $65,000 purchase to stand out for all to see was the shape of the base Corvette's 1992 tail—a narrower version of the unique 1990 ZR1, so now only the wider rear wheels and the roof-mounted high-level brake light helped quick identification of the super-car. Apart from the changes common to all 1991s, only a valet key, which automatically reverted to off, was new for the ZR1.

Traction control, ASR, was new across the Corvette range but it was particularly welcome for the ZR1, since it allowed much more frequent use of the right pedal. Sales were down to just 504, not helped by the extra 50 horsepower now enjoyed by the base LT1 engine of the standard car.

The last LT5 motor was assembled at Stillwater in November 1993, after enough had been built to sell a

further 448 cars in each of the three years through 1995, and to keep a supply for warranty claims. The last 20 or so of these were released for sale by GM Parts Division as crate motors during 2000. Spurred by the more powerful LT1 and a 395 horsepower claim for the 10-cylinder Chrysler Viper, the 1993 and later motors were modified to give 405 horsepower. The main bearing cradle was made stronger and redesigned for four-bolt retention, heads were ported and matched to the intake plenum, and the camshaft was revised.

At last the ZR1 was allowed to look distinctly different from the standard car, with a superb new set of five-spoke alloy wheels. Called A-molds by enthusiasts, who quickly bought them to retro-fit to earlier Corvettes, they were the first five-spokes ever made for the car. With only 448 cars sold for each of the last three years of production, and with the extra 30bhp, these are the rarest and most collectible of the series.

Above: 1995 ZR1 with 405 bhp and 5-spoke wheels.

Left: The 1990 ZR1 LT5 engine was rated at 375 hp for 1990–1992.

SPECIFICATIONS

Wheel-base 104.52"
Length 15' 0"
Width 6' 10" (including mirrors)
Weight 3245 lbs
Transmission 4-speed auto
   or 6-speed manual
Brakes 13" front
   12" rear
Engine LS1 350 V8
Compression 10.0
Net Horse Power 345
Max Torque 350 lb-ft

1997

The new model Corvette that was eventually released in January 1997 was the most eagerly anticipated new model ever. Finally presented simultaneously on stage at the Detroit and Los Angeles Auto Shows, no one was disappointed by the superb new shape, and the technical specification and performance figures presented with it. It was the fastest, widest, sleekest, most fuel-efficient Corvette ever, with the most legroom, the best seats, the most luggage area and the best fit and finish ever.

There had been plenty of time to get it right. The new model was originally to have been a 1993, but political and financial turmoil within GM, following declining market share for their disappointing bread-and-butter passenger cars and near bankruptcy for the Corporation in 1991, nearly saw development curtailed, and even the flagship sports car cancelled forever. These extraordinary times were well documented by the late James Schefter in his 1997 book *All Corvette are Red*, and by the Corvette Chief Engineer himself, Dave McLellan in his 2002 *Corvette from the Inside*. Without any doubt, a loyal band of designers and engineers, in particular stylist John Cafaro and McLellan, devoted to the heritage of the Corvette and believing in their future in a revived General Motors, bent the rules and fought to save their baby.

The years spent in refining and developing the car show through in every aspect of the design. Remove the door panel of a 1984 C4 Corvette, and there is a mass of cables for the speakers, window motor, power door locks, mirror heat and adjustment, interior lamp, wiper switch, courtesy lamp switch and hatch release switch, together with multiple brackets and stampings to support all of these, plus the window regulator. Remove the door panel from a 1997, and by comparison there is a void, an empty space with a supremely simple and effective window

regulator and room to hide a change of clothes and a wash bag. This was partly due to the use of solid-state door modules to control the functions and replace much of the wiring seen in the 1984, but it was mainly rigorous design discipline that ensured that no bracket or support could be included unless it was essential and served many functions. The same philosophy ran right through the car, and is particularly obvious to those who repair Corvettes in the front bumper, where the endless cheap stamped brackets, supports, spacers, retainers and bolts of the 1984–1996 car, which took more than a page to list, were replaced by a few well-designed components that could be written on a shirt cuff.

This approach helped to make the better-equipped and much more sophisticated C5 into a lighter and much less rattle-ridden car than its predecessor. We now know that a late design change to the 1984 forced the removal of a C3 style central longitudinal roof bar, a decision that seriously compromised its structural stiffness, but management was determined that, with the roof panel removed, there should be an unimpeded upward view. At the time of design it was probably not intended that there should be a convertible version of the Corvette, but fashions change and those most likely to remove the targa roof could chose the open top model from 1986. To keep some stiffness in the 1984 coupe, the roof had to be bolted into place at each corner—making removal into a six-minute task rather than a 20-second unclip.

Early on in the C5 design process it was decided that, after forty years of too flexible chassis designs, the new Corvette would now set an industry standard for torsional stiffness. A frame based on two hydro-formed rails was the answer. The structure based on this new and expensive technology was strong enough to allow a fully-open targa roof for the fiberglass bodied car with an unstressed panel or convertible roof, while still retaining the stiffness of a fully-roofed steel body.

The profile of the first buyer was now considered to have changed. Lengthening the wheelbase by more than 8 inches to 104.5 inches, from a previous 96.2 inches, gave much more interior space, and improved high speed stability, but inevitably reduced the quick steering response that gave the C4 its kart-like feel. The steering wheel was slightly increased in diameter and reduced on center gearing too, perhaps reflecting a view that the Corvette was now targeted at an older buyer. To be fair this was

more noticeable to European buyers facing endless corners and roundabouts, but was also perceived by any American making a right turn at a stoplight.

Unlike the three previous changeovers of 1963, 1968 and 1984, when the base motor was transferred unaltered to the new model, the new 1997 had an entirely new engine, and almost every other part of the car was new too. Normally some minor items, such as clutch thrust bearings or tire valves, would be expected to continue, but even the latter were new, integrated into Irish-made, radio-transmitting pressure sensors for the new on-screen tire monitor system.

Known as the LS1, the new Generation III all-aluminum 5.7 liter small block had almost nothing, apart from its capacity, in common with its 1955–1996 iron block predecessor. It was 44 pounds lighter than LT1, 45 horsepower more powerful and built in Romulus, Michigan rather than the traditional factory at Flint where all

previous Corvette small blocks had been sourced. Even the firing order of 1-8-7-2-6-5-4-3 was new, replacing 1-8-4-3-6-5-7-2, which could suffer mixture starvation from the proximity of the adjacent cylinders 5 and 7 firing so closely. The new firing order gave an interesting exhaust sound at idle—too much for some owners, who bought cross-over kits to Siamese their true dual exhaust systems and restore the traditional smooth burble. Escaping the LT1's ill-placed, front-mounted distributor, the ignition system now used a crankshaft trigger, and each plug had its own coil mounted above the valve cover.

The only possible parts in common with the C5 were the internal components of the 4L60E automatic transmission, which had an entirely new external case because it was now moved to the back of the car in front of the axle, making space for two full sized footwells, and even a rest for the driver's left foot. The prop shaft was now an enclosed torque tube, something not seen in a Chevrolet for more than fifty years. Six-speed manual transmission was now an $815 option.

Standard wheels were five-spoke aluminum, 17-inch x 8-inch front and 18-inch x 9-inch rear. They carried P245/45 ZR17 and P275/40 ZR18 Goodyear Eagle EMT tires, there being no spare wheel on the car. An optional light-weight magnesium wheel made by Speedline of Italy was fitted to export cars, when it was found that the slight protrusion of the wheels from the arches by the aluminum wheels contravened regulations in some European countries. These were offered in 1998 as a $3000 option on home market cars too. The export cars were very well received around the world and featured a 300mph speedometer face, which was designed to accommodate the full sweep of the needle at the Corvette's maximum speed of 290kph when the gauges were switched to metric. Whatever the reason, a 300mph speedo impresses English schoolboys like nothing else! Export cars featured

additional fog lamps in the tail, a larger rear license plate aperture, and tail lamps incorporating amber turn signal sectors on the outer, and back-up sectors on the inner lamps. Chevrolet went to great length to make the car acceptable in foreign countries, incorporating all the correct international markings on critical items such as glass and seat belts, and ensuring that the car complied with the myriad technical requirements.

Opposite Top: The Long wheelbase and great aerodynamics make the C5 Corvette superbly stable, even at its 187mph top speed.

Opposite Bottom: Sleek body work conceals a state of the art chassis.

Top: The entire engine compartment is styled to match the 345hp LS5.

Bottom: At last a Corvette with space to spare for the tallest driver.

SPECIFICATIONS

Wheel-base 104.52"
Length 15' 0"
Width 6' 10" (including mirrors)
Weight 3245 lbs
Transmission 4-speed auto
  or 6-speed manual
Brakes 13" front
  12" rear
Engine LS1 350 V8
Compression 10.0
Net Horse Power 345
Max Torque 350 lb-ft

1998

1998 saw the introduction of the new convertible, which immediately accounted for a third of production, while the trend for the C4 had been that they never exceeded a quarter of the total. The design was particularly exciting, with the rear deck tumbling down between the seats in a manner reminiscent of the first generation cars. The convertible top design was excellent too, manually operated and completely hidden below the deck panel as it had been since 1953, but now—instead of rear latches—an internal tensioning system that pressed the rear bow against the deck as the front latches were tightened. That this model had the smallest back window of any Corvette ever didn't seem to bother anyone—at least it was glass and heated.

The new convertible, which commanded a $6,930 premium, was given an added boost by being selected for the fourth time as the pace car for the 1998 Indianapolis 500 race. The chosen color scheme was the most outrageous yet, Pace Car Purple exterior, with Yellow wheels and decals, and a black and yellow leather interior. The convertible tops were black cloth. Once again the combination worked, and a total of 1,163 of the $5,039.00 option were built. At a total of $49,464, this was the most expensive Corvette convertible ever.

One of the most appealing features of the convertible was its separate trunk, the first since 1962. While still allowing reach through access from the seating area, it could accommodate two golf bags, even with the top stowed, and could be remotely opened with the key fob.

Every Corvette crash is a tragedy, and anything that can help prevent accidents helps us all. Apart from the personal pain and suffering of injured occupants and the

cost of repairs to the car, there is the knock-on effect to all our insurance premiums, so any accident-prevention system built into the Corvette benefits us all. For 1998, Active Handling offered the next level of driver assistance and electronic accident prevention, in the hierarchy that had commenced with ABS in 1986 and went on to ASR traction control in 1992. Now JL4 Active Handling brought true yaw control to the option list, for only $500. A yaw rate sensor compared the steering wheel angle, forward speed and the actual turning rate of the vehicle. If the yaw rate was beyond anticipated parameters, the vehicle was under-steering or over-steering—sliding its front or rear wheels—and the yaw control would then intervene by applying appropriate braking to individual wheels, to rebalance the car and set it back on the course intended by the driver in his steering input. A console-mounted switch allowed the system to be switched off for track days or gymkhana driving, when a more exuberant driving style might be required.

Top: New for 1998 was the convertible, with a top that locked into raised position with just the two front catchers.

Above: The Indianapolis 500 replica; raised headrest fairings identify this as one of the cars used at the event.

SPECIFICATIONS

Wheel-base 104.52"
Length 15' 0"
Width 6' 10" (including mirrors)
Weight 3245 lbs
Transmission 4-speed auto
   or 6-speed manual
Brakes 13" front
   12" rear
Engine LS1 350 V8
Compression 10.0
Net Horse Power 345
Max Torque 350 lb-ft

1999

Determined to keep innovation happening and achieve the usual full coverage in the automotive Press, for 1999 the long discussed Hard-top was announced. Not the bare bones, no-frills, vinyl-seated lightweight that had sometimes been discussed, but nevertheless the cheapest model by $394, this fixed-roof model completed the planned three car Corvette C5 range. Close in concept to the hard-top-only cars of 1956 to 1967, when the hard-top could be substituted for the soft-top, the new model went a stage further by bonding the fiberglass hard-top directly onto the open car. This resulted in the stiffest structure of any Corvette so far. With a strongly sporting emphasis, six-speed manual and the hard Z51 suspension were included in the base price. Seats were in black leather only, with the option of power for the driver only, and exterior color choice was limited too.

A new feature for 1999, which quickly became a must-have option and brought buyers of earlier C5s back to their dealers to trade up, was Head Up Display (HUD). Using aircraft technology, essential gauge displays were projected onto a special windshield, and focussed so that the blue screen appeared to be placed a foot or so above the front bumper. Corvettes have a magnetic attraction for law enforcement officers, and a digital speed display in the line of sight makes compliance to the maximum permissible speed, while being followed, a stress-free experience. Simple controls varied height, brightness and the content of the page, which could be as different as digital speed only, for critical suburban roads, or just tachometer and oil pressure for track use.

Telescopic steering columns, a popular option since 1965, were combined with tilt in 1969, and had been a standard feature since 1980. They were eliminated by the needs of the airbag in 1990, though the tilt feature was retained. Now the telescopic column returned as an option for 1999, for the coupe and convertible only, this time electrically powered.

Twilight Sentinel had been a feature of GM sister division Cadillac since the seventies, using a photo-electric cell and time delays to switch on lights automatically. This at last became a Corvette option too. While soon taken for granted on your own 'Vette, the downside is that every other car you drive infuriates by not having automatic lights on too!

Below: Standard aluminum wheels were much more durable than the $3000 optional magnesium.

Top: This Export C5 has side repeater lamps, Italian made Speedline magnesium wheels, optional on US cars, amber rear side markers, special rear lamps and rear fog lamps cut into the rear fascia.

Above: Front of Export car shows additional white front parking lights and European standard towing loop.

SPECIFICATIONS

Wheel-base 104.52"
Length 15' 0"
Width 6' 10" (including mirrors)
Weight 3245 lbs
Transmission 4-speed auto
  or 6-speed manual
Brakes 13" front
  12" rear
Engine LS1 350 V8
Compression 10.0
Net Horse Power 345
Max Torque 350 lb-ft

2000

A new model had been launched in each of the three preceding years of the C5, but for the 2000 Millennium year only, a new color, Millennium Yellow, made the headlines. Using a tinted clear coat, rather than clear, helped to give this $500 option color an exceptional depth. The yellow was similar to that used on the C5R racing Corvettes, which were starting to make a good impression in Endurance races such as the Sebring 12 hour, and the Daytona and Le Mans 24 hour races. Otherwise the car was subject to a series of detail improvements, such as better seat materials, improved seat belts with guides to prevent the belts twisting on retraction, a brighter Torch Red to replace the previous Firethorn for the interior, and improved side window seals.

Passive Keyless Entry (PKE), a popular standard feature since 1993, was surprisingly dropped and at the same time the key barrel for the passenger side was removed too. PKE was never an option for export cars,

SPECIFICATIONS

Wheel-base 104.52"
Length 15' 0"
Width 6' 10" (including mirrors)
Weight 3245 lbs
Transmission 4-speed auto
   or 6-speed manual
Brakes 13" front
   12" rear
Engine LS1 350 V8
Compression 10.0
Net Horse Power 350
Max Torque 350 lb-ft

Optional Z06 350 V8
Net Horse Power 385
Max Torque 385 lb-ft

2001

because the radio frequency was not cleared for automotive use in some countries.

The thick spoke base aluminum road wheel was replaced by an elegant thin spoke design, optionally polished for an additional $895. The amazingly expensive bronze-colored magnesium optional wheel, made in Italy by Speedline, was reduced by $1000 to just $2000.

Guaranteed to make a major impact around the world, the new Z06 was based on the Hard-top model that it now replaced. Rated at 385 horsepower, more than

the 1990–1992 ZR1, the new engine was designated LS6 after the rare 425hp aluminum-headed big block of 1971. The body was distinguished by stainless steel front bumper air grilles, functional rear brake duct inlets behind the doors, red brake calipers and unique wheels. These were wider than the coupe and convertible wheels by one inch, and carried Goodyear Eagle Supercar tires without run-flat capability. Because there was no spare wheel either, a motorcycle-style tire inflation kit was supplied in case of a puncture. Exterior colors were limited as with

Right Top: The lower opening ducts cold air to front brakes. White bulb export parking lamps have been added to this car for UK use.

Right Center: All C5 Corvettes have world standard flip back mirrors.

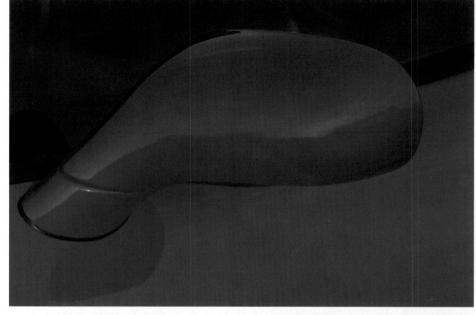

Right Bottom: The LS1 engine is placed well back, thanks to rear mounted transmission, giving excellent weight distribution.

SPECIFICATIONS

Wheel-base 104.52"
Length 15' 0"
Width 6' 10" (including mirrors)
Weight 3245 lbs
Transmission 4-speed auto
  or 6-speed manual
Brakes 13" front
  12" rear
Engine LS1 350 V8
Compression 10.0
Net Horse Power 350
Max Torque 350 lb-ft

Optional Z06 350 V8
Net Horse Power 405
Max Torque 400 lb-ft

2002

the previous Hard-top, and the interior was black, or black and red. The tachometer was redlined at 6500rpm rather than the 6000 of the LS1.

The coupe and convertible's LS1 shared the revised block design of the LS6, and gained an extra engine 5 horsepower to be rated at 350. Both were now built at St. Catherines, Ontario in Canada. Because the Hard-top had become the Z06, the Coupe was once again the cheapest Corvette.

Not content with being the most powerful single-cam Chevrolet small block yet, the LS6 engine of the Z06 was now rated at 405 horsepower—pointedly the same as the final three years of the ZR1, and the most powerful 5.7 liter production Corvette ever. To make the most of this, the side emblems of the Z06 now incorporated the figures 405. The extra power was achieved by eliminating two pre-cats in the exhaust system, improving intake airflow, and an extra high-lift cam, combined with lighter-weight valves. The intake valves were hollow, as were the exhaust valves, but filled with potassium and sodium alloy

for better heat transfer, a technique used in high performance motorcycles for almost fifty years.

All models now broke the $40,000 barrier, but the 2002 Corvette that received the most media coverage was not for sale at any price. For the fifth time Corvette was chosen to pace the Indianapolis 500, a race which in 2002 would be dominated by Chevrolet engines, with 14 of the 15 finishers—including the three podium cars—thus powered. Previous Pace Cars had been Corvettes in 1978, 1986, 1995 and 1998—all available as replicas with appropriate decals. But for 2002, only three were built and none for public sale. All three were in fact prototypes for the 2003 50th anniversary car, with additional 50th and Indy 500 decals.

SPECIFICATIONS

Wheel-base 104.52"
Length 15' 0"
Width 6' 10" (including mirrors)
Weight 3245 lbs
Transmission 4-speed auto
   or 6-speed manual
Brakes 13" front
   12" rear
Engine LS1 350 V8
Compression 10.0
Net Horse Power 350
Max Torque 350 lb-ft

Optional ZO6 350 V8
Net Horse Power 405
Max Torque 400 lb-ft

2003

Because the 1983 Corvette was never built, but instead the 1984 followed the 1982 after a five-month hiatus, the 2003 is the 50th and not the 51st model, which it would otherwise have been with production starting in 1953.

The 50th Anniversary Corvette was available as a Coupe or Convertible, in a special 50th Red with gold-tinted Champagne wheels and a two-tone Shale leather interior. Included with all Anniversary models was the new F55 Selective Magnetic Ride Control. Like F45, this used a microprocessor to measure the vertical movement of each wheel every millisecond. Using a new damper technology from GM Delphi, a magnetic field varied the viscosity of a special synthetic oil, in which very small iron particles were suspended. This enabled the ride to be varied for every half-inch of road traveled at 60mph.

All Corvettes have been fiberglass-bodied two-seaters, almost all have been pure convertibles or had removable roof panels, and all but the first two years of production have been V8 powered. More than 1,250,000 Corvettes have been made, making it by far the most popular 2-seater sports car, and the most numerous fiberglass bodied vehicle ever built—and because of its stout construction there are still more Corvettes around than any other sports car. Roll on the C6!

Above: The convertible seat divider treatment recalls 1953-62; it is also the first open Corvette since then with a trunk.

Below: 2003 Z06

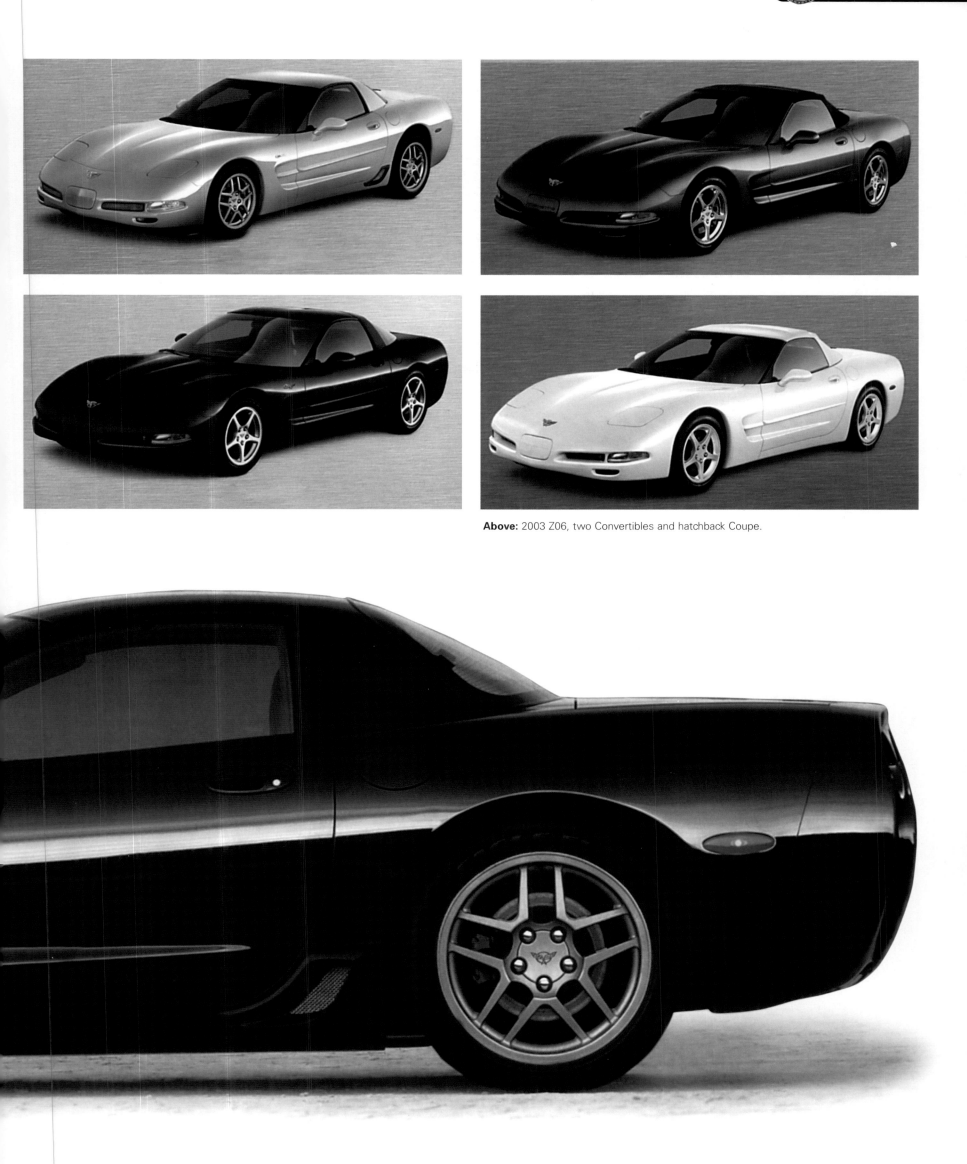

Above: 2003 Z06, two Convertibles and hatchback Coupe.

Above: 2003 50th Anniversary.

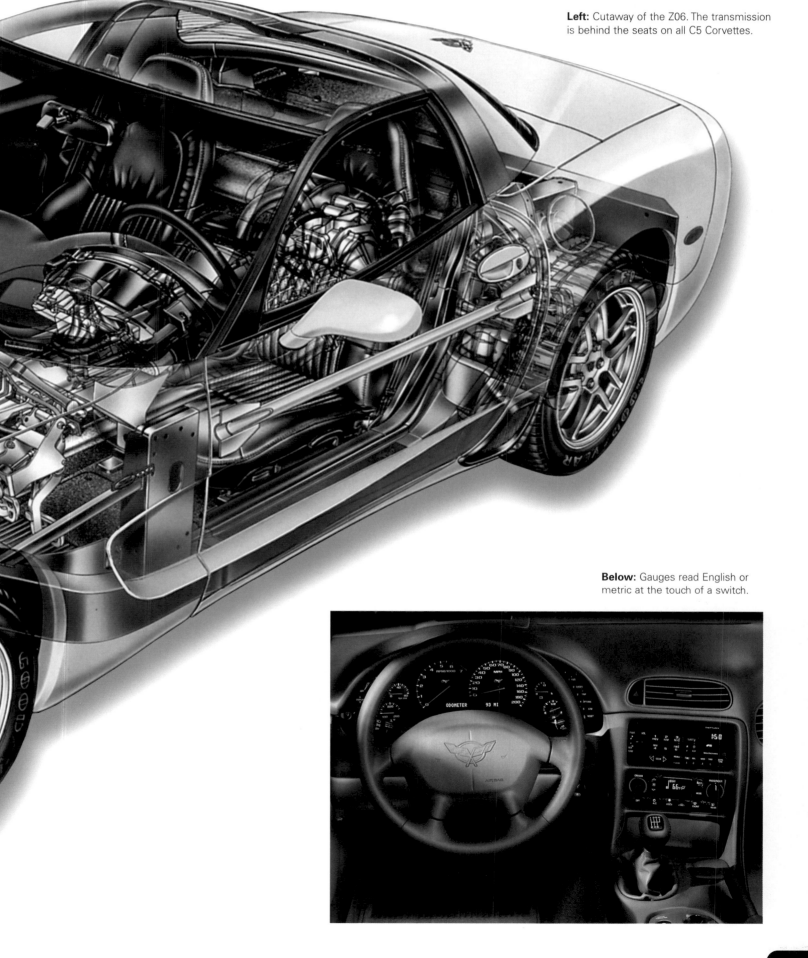

Left: Cutaway of the Z06. The transmission is behind the seats on all C5 Corvettes.

Below: Gauges read English or metric at the touch of a switch.

Credits

Special thanks are due to Fred Mullauer and the members of the Mason Dixon Chapter of the National Corvette Restorers Society who allowed their cars to be photographed and in particular

C1 – Tony Avedisian, Chuck Berge, Chuck Gongloff, John Grath, Steve Lesser, Don Loveless, Jay Matricciani, Dennis Moore, Jim Moran, Fred Mullauer, Mike Shepard, Steve Sokoloff, Doug Sonders, and Tony Zagorski.

C2 – Gary Barnes, Dick Benton, Chuck Gongloff, Rudy Gonzalez, Ron Goralski, Steve Hafner, Udo Horn, Don Hyson, Irwin Kroiz, Steve Lesser, Mike Lienard, George McNab, Mark Mehl, Dennis Moore, Butch Moxley, Fred Mullauer, Trevor Rogers, Eric Thomas, Bill Thompson, Chuck Walker, Mark Wilson and John Wright.

C3 – Herb Abdill, Pete Alatzas, Tony Avedisian, Bill Benton, Dick Benton, Chuck Berge, Ken Brown, Bill Fink, Jerry Fink, Rick Gondeck, Pat Gongloff, John Hock, Tim Humphreys, Kim Jordan, Larry Kupka, Bill McVeigh, Ray Morrison, Butch Moxley, Mike Moxley, James Pasko, Duane Ravenberg, Lee Sherman, Frank Stech, Michael Streckfus and Andrew Toman. In the UK thanks to friends and fellow club members.

C4 – Bruce Evans, Russell Hayman, Brian Neighbour, Stephen Ouvaroff at the American Carriage Company, Kingston upon Thames, David Rees-Williams, Paul Sword, Bill Wilkins.

C5 – Nick Barattieri, Gordon Broadley, Tony Cohen at American Car Imports London, Keith Jewell, Mel Visconti, John Wells, Ian Wilson.

And the various unknown owners of the Corvettes photographed for Chrysalis Images, which we have been fortunate to access. Special thanks too to Fred Mullauer, the staff at Rogers Corvette Center in Maitland, Florida and at Claremont Corvette in Snodland, England. Over many years the author has been privileged to have had long discussions with Bill Mitchell, Larry Shinoda and Zora Arkus-Duntov, all now sadly departed, and Dave McLellan, Chuck Jordan, Reeves Callaway, Dave Hill, Jim Hall, Gib Hufstader and Gordon Killebrew all who have contributed by their knowledge and enthusiasm to this book.

Corvette is a big subject and has attracted some great writers. The author acknowledges the work of and is indebted in particular to Noland Adams, Karl Ludvigsen and Michael Antonick as well as Alan Colvin, Anthony Young, John Amgwert and the late James Schefter.

And with thanks to my editor, Marie Clayton, and designer, Chris Bladon.

Picture Credits

All pictures copyright © Chrysalis Images except for the following:

James Mann

7 bottom, 13 top, 16-7, 18-9, 22-3, 24-5, 28-9, 40, 42-3, 46-7, 48-9, 50-1, 52, 53 bottom, 58-9, 60 top, 62-3, 64-5, 66-7, 70-1, 72-3, 76-7, 78-9 bottom, 79, 80-1, 82-3, 84-5, 86-7, 88-9, 90-1, 92-3, 94-5. 96-7, 98-9, 106-7, 110, 120-1, 122-3, 124-5, 126-7, 128-9, 130-1, 132-3, 134-5, 136-7, 142-3, 146-7, 148-9, 150-1, 154-5

Classic & Sports Car Magazine, London

118-9

Courtesy of Chevrolet Division of General Motors

8-9, 141 top right, 152-3, 156-7, 158-9